Guide to the wines of
Burgundy

GRAHAM CHIDGEY

Series Editor
Pamela Vandyke Price

PITMAN

PITMAN PUBLISHING LIMITED
39 Parker Street, London WC2B 5PB

Associated Companies
Copp Clarke Ltd, Toronto
Fearon-Pitman Publishers Inc, Belmont, California
Pitman Publishing Co. SA (Pty) Ltd, Johannesburg
Pitman Publishing New Zealand Ltd, Wellington
Pitman Publishing Pty Ltd, Melbourne

Text set in 10/11 pt Photon Baskerville, printed by photolithography and bound in Great Britain at The Pitman Press, Bath.

ISBN 0 273 01043 3

Contents

Acknowledgements

In preparing my first book on wine after twenty-five years spent as a trainee, salesman, buyer, merchant and shipper, I am now well convinced that writing is another matter. Without the assistance of Mrs. Pamela Vandyke Price this little effort would never have reached the publisher, which places me considerably in her debt.

Three lovely ladies have variously helped me along the way and I thank them for their patient typing—Jane Fripp, Mollie Berwick and Helen Thomson.

All the authors listed in the Bibliography have been referred to at great length and I am fortunate in my distinguished predecessors. Yet most information has come from the time spent in the company of Pierre Maufoux of Santenay, a real master of the Art of Burgundy wines.

The cover photograph was taken by Patrick Eager.

Foreword

Writers of many books dealing with wine for the benefit of the traveller do, in my opinion, tend to be somewhat dogmatic about what the wines are like. Yet is it helpful to give a single sentence of generalization—and possibly risk puzzling the reader, whose experiences of trying these particular wines may result in his forming a totally contrary opinion? On the other hand, too much detail about the wines of a quite small region can be bewildering.

There is no one way to overcome this difficulty. I know that some travellers like to have a definite guideline as to the general character of the wines of a particular village. But others prefer to try and form their own opinions. Yet, if you have only a short time available, you may never encounter an absolutely typical wine, and go away wondering why I should have described it in a particular way. The only thing to hope is that no lover of wine will be put off by one disappointment, any more than he will be foolish enough to form a fixed opinion of a wine as the result of one single fortunate experience of it.

Fine Burgundy is a minority group in the world of wine, and therefore I think that dogmatic assertions of quality are valueless—indeed, unwise.

Take nothing for granted in Burgundy. Just because the name on a label is well-known, because it is that of a sought-after and much publicised *appellation*, don't automatically assume that the wine will be great. Just because a shipper has established the name of his establishment in the minds of the public, don't think that you, personally, will always find every single one of his wines to your liking, or even falling into line with the standards of quality you form after a little experience. But don't, either, reject the chance to try a wine because you may not have heard of the name, or the shipper.

Try many different wines, from different shippers. Find a wine merchant who shares your love of Burgundy and who will frankly admire even the wines of his competitors when these are good. Such a source of supply will certainly prove a friend.

1

Burgundy

The vineyards are still very much a family business. It is the members of the families who, throughout the year, work hard and steadily among their vines, sometimes assisted by other workers and, at vintage time, large numbers of pickers hired for the occasion—university students, travelling workers from Spain, Italy and Portugal, plus a regular flow of trainee wine-trade students. It is quite usual for a Burgundian to be in full time employment in a shop, office or business completely separate from wine, but to work in the family plot either before or after his normal day's occupation. The children are not spared, and learn the wine routines from an early age.

Burgundy remains one of the few French wine regions where all but the finest growths are produced by small farmers, from vineyards cultivated in very much the same tradition as in centuries past, and only recently has the routine altered significantly from the practices understood by the great-great-great-grandparents of the growers you meet and see today.

Vineyard holdings are very small indeed. Some estates may be as large as 40 hectares in total, spread over many different vineyards, or as small as 3 hectares. It is said a family can live very well off 3 hectares as long as the holding is within one of the finest *appellations*. Normally a family or *domaine* (estate) will own plots of vineyards that have been acquired, over many years, following a shrewd marriage settlement, or from the apportionment of vineyards after the proprietor's death.

The *domaines* owned by the shippers will be managed by a specialist member of the firm, and they will have cellars available in the villages of their interest; the small family grower, however, will probably own just one cellar, this being either adjacent to his house or nearby in his village, and this is where all the grapes will be brought at harvest time.

Grapes from within the same *appellation contrôlée* region may be pressed and fermented together, but of course grapes from individual vineyards and different *appellations* are kept separately by law. Therefore, within a cellar there may be several

Underground cellar for storing young wines in casks

different wines for A.O.C. (*appellation contrôlée*) purposes.

This is the main reason why Burgundies that are entitled to be labelled '*Mise du domaine*' or 'Domaine bottled' are not actually bottled in the vineyard where the grapes are grown (unless this happens to coincide with the location of the owner's cellar) but in the proprietor's cellars, which may be in a quite different, and possibly even fairly distant, village. For example, a Volnay may be labelled as 'domaine bottled' when the *domaine* where it is bottled is at Pommard; the wine has been made at this *domaine*, and the description is therefore correct.

The Importance of Bottling

Until comparatively recently, most Burgundy was bottled by the shipper or merchant in the place or country to which the wine was sold. This is still done with the cheaper wines, and they may be admirably handled by firms with experience in this skilled task and the equipment necessary to ensure that the wine is kept in perfect condition. But lately there has grown a vogue for *domaine* bottling by certain markets and customers, and some of those who insist on it often maintain that the resulting wine is better, and the bottling itself more skilled. In fact, there is no such guarantee logically associated with a *domaine*-bottled wine. Some *domaines* care for and bottle their wines extremely well—others do not.

When *domaine* bottling is bad, it is very bad, but the *négociant* (shipper) who does the bottling may have other faults too. It is prudent to analyse any Burgundy before it is bottled, primarily to check that the wine really has finished its malo-lactic fermentation and that this is not lying dormant in the wine; often bottlers do not check this and later on, after the wine has gone into bottle, it starts 'working' or fermenting again—something that can be detected by the presence of minuscule bubbles at the edge of the wine in the glass and the slightly 'prickly' sensation that will be noted on the tongue. This malo-lactic fermentation, is something that lasts only for a short time—possibly only a few days—and is quite normal in the wine's development: the wine must get through this stage before it is bottled, otherwise it will never be quite right.

Something that definitely affects the wine-loving traveller in Burgundy as a result of the increased popularity of *domaine* bottling, is that *domaine*-bottled wines may be offered for sale to the itinerant holiday maker at very fancy prices; the trade buying will be more alert to the quality of wines offered in this way, but the tourist may get something that is both expensive and hardly worth buying anyway. On a recent visit I paid to Pommard, I noted that one grower, who would have sold his ordinary Bourgogne Rouge to me at a fairly modest price, was charging nearly three times as much for exactly the same wine to those who hope to purchase something '*domaine*-bottled at the *domaine*'.

As far as *domaine*-bottled Burgundies bought by U.K. shippers are concerned, the majority of these will have been bought by the British firm's buying direct from the *domaine*. As I have said, until recently most U.K. firms received their Burgundies in bulk, in cask, and bottled the wines themselves, but the stricter application of the laws of A.O.C. now means that the majority of the fine wines are and indeed have to be bottled in the area of production. But of course, an original bottled wine will inevitably be more expensive on any export market, because of the greater expense in handling in bottle rather than in bulk, and because it pays a slightly higher duty.

However, the increase in *domaine* bottling has caused some shippers in Burgundy to make deals with vineyard owners, either agreeing to do the distribution of the wine for them, or to buy the whole of the crop—an obvious advantage as far as the small proprietor is concerned. So, if the *vigneron* or owner does not bottle his own wine, he has to find a buyer among the shippers.

The Broker and the Commissionaire en Vins

The way the grower does this is to make use of a broker (*courtier de campagne*). This broker will earn a commission of 2 per cent from the shipper on what he arranges for the *vigneron* to sell, and, if he can, another 2 per cent from the *vigneron* as well; he lives solely by his commissions and does not hold stocks of wine. But these courtiers are usually highly specialised dealers in wine, knowing exactly the various wines of different villages and cultivating a working relationship with the growers, as well as the shippers. They can, thereby, save the shippers a great deal of time because of their ability, as it were, to pre-select the stocks that they know a particular shipper will want to buy.

If a well-established *courtier* does acquire some stock of wines, he is known as a *commissionnaire en vins*. But he will not hold this stock in his own cellars. He will keep it—usually only for a short time—in the cellars of the grower, and he will sell it as soon as possible, charging a commission of about 5 per cent.

Shippers and Agents

The *négociant* (shipper) will have large cellars, in which the wines he has bought may be stored for maturation and eventually bottled. Many of these cellars are open to visitors and a guided tour of at least one is essential for the lover of Burgundy.

What the *négociant*'s job consists of is to supply the wine merchants who buy from him, and to sell the wines he holds either under his own label, or label them for the purchaser. Obviously, substantial stocks of wine are essential for the *négociant* to maintain continuity of his particular 'house style' of a range of wines; quantities are often required far in excess of those village wines that the *négociant* has been able to buy himself direct from individual growers. So the buyer of the establishment will buy in various lots from the required A.O.C.s, and the wines will be blended in the cellars of the shipper. This process, known as '*assemblage*', is a skilled task, requiring much experience, in order that the shipper can maintain the house style that he has found his customers like. The merchant who will buy the wines (or the restaurant, hotel chain, or similar organisation) will also know the wine his clientele prefers.

This is why the name of the house is of such importance when choosing Burgundy—the wines of one establishment may be perfectly good but quite unlike those of another, which are equally good. And the continuity is something of which the purchaser must be assured: obviously, no customer wants to select and ship a light, fruity Beaune, for example, only to find that, when he re-orders that wine (having found that his public like it as much as he does) that the wine, albeit selling under the same name, is now a fat, overweight type of Beaune. This is why style control is so important and why certain styles have, over the years, become associated with certain establishments.

Some *négociants,* in times of prosperity, bought vineyards for themselves. For example, in the A.O.C. Beaune area, there are more shippers owning vineyards than *vignerons:* Chanson Père et Fils, Bouchard Père et Fils, Joseph Drouhin, Louis Latour and Jaboulet Vercherre are substantial proprietors.

It would be impossible for a Burgundy shipper to cover all the export markets with whom he deals from Burgundy itself: even if, physically, he had the staff to do so, the expense involved would make the ultimate price of the wine even higher. So he often appoints an agent in each of his main markets.

This agent may sometimes be one person, but usually consists of a firm experienced in that market, who will be handling other wines, but of course not those that are in direct competition with those of the shipper. Rather confusingly, such a firm, if it deals with supplying the wine trade rather than doing business directly with the public, is also known in the U.K. as a 'shipper'; but the firm may, in a few instances, be doing business as a merchant as well, and have arranged an exclusivity for the wines of a particular Burgundy house, which sell these within a specific area.

There are also the big shippers who own retail chains, offlicences and hotels and restaurant groups, as well as controlling public houses or outlets such as the railways. But the smaller firms, which may enjoy outstanding prestige, can be equally important, especially as regards certain wines that are never available in vast quantities because only small amounts are made. This is why you may see the name of a particular Burgundy shipper in a number of different places even in the U.K.—the establishment has arranged to sell the way that seems most strategically effective, and immediately profitable.

U.K. agents for the main Burgundy houses may have been associated with the establishments they represent for generations, or they may be creating a new market for a particular house. They have a stiff task at the present time, when Burgundy prices, even for the more ordinary wines, are rising sharply and some of the cherished names are now in a price bracket that seems beyond decency. However, the buyer of a bottle of Burgundy is getting the 'real thing' to a greater extent than he might have done before regulations were tightened up. This means that the true style of the fine Burgundies can be shown and speak for itself.

There is no doubt this improvement in the moral standards throughout Burgundy and the virtual abolition of foreign bottling of *appellation* (A.C.) wines has contributed to the inflationary spiral of prices facing the Burgundy buyer.

Wine Fraternities of Burgundy

CONFRERIE DES CHEVALIERS DU TASTEVIN

In the forty-odd years since its inception in 1934, the Chevaliers du Tastevin* have become legendary. Joining the Order is much sought after, if only because members qualify for regular dining in the most splendid and imposing surroundings of the

---

* Confrérie des Chevaliers du Tastevin. Address enquiries to: The Secretary, La Confrérie des Chevaliers du Tastevin, 21 Nuits St. Georges.

Clos de Vougeot. Membership does not, however, mean that the member is an outstanding authority on Burgundy.

The founders of the Confrérie were Camille Rodier and Georges Faiveley, both of whom were deeply involved in the Burgundy area and its wines between the wars, when the whole trade was depressed by a succession of poor vintages and world-wide recession. The Chevaliers du Tastevin grew slowly in numbers until 1944, when they purchased the buildings of the Clos de Vougeot and began a dedicated programme of restoration of the great buildings to their former brilliance. Much of the funds required then and since have been donated by associated Chapters abroad—notably the U.S.A.

Ceremonial dress of senior Members of Chevaliers du Tastevin at Clos de Vougeot

It is widely believed that membership of the Chevaliers du Tastevin is restricted to members of the wine, restaurant and hotel trade, but this is not exactly so, as membership embraces the arts, commerce and science on an international level.

There are twenty or so meetings per year, when between 500 and 600 people will sit down to a gastronomic banquet. The atmosphere of these dinners epitomises France's love of '*les belles choses*' (the good things of life: food and drink). By no means all members are wealthy, as sensible arrangements are made for a true cross-section of people from all walks of Burgundian life.

To visit Clos de Vougeot is a 'must' for any visitor. There are remnants of the original sixteenth-century buildings. The process of wine-making is described by guides, who provide a complete history of its foundation by the Cistercian Order.

As a further extension of their authority, the Chevaliers du Tastevin instituted a system of 'wine approval' for Burgundy wines in 1950. According to this, any grower or *négociant* can present his wine to a special committee, free of charge, when it will be judged according to its vintage and *appellation* at a 'blind' tasting—price is not mentioned. If approval is given, the Chevaliers du Tastevin sell to the applicant their specially designed labels, which are numbered to the quantity of bottles declared; this definitely enhances the prestige and value of the wine, at least in France, certain export markets and many smart restaurants. Successful wines are then described as *Tastevine*.

It is interesting to find that many writers on wine suggest that this scrutiny of samples by the Chevaliers is quite severe. I am sure that this may be so, but in my tasting experience too many borderline cases have been approved and I would prefer to see a strengthening of the quality standards if the system is to be taken seriously by the consumer. At present about one in two of the wines presented seems to pass this test. The promotional activities for Burgundy and its wines achieved by the Chevaliers du Tastevin have been quite outstanding and deserve the applause of all wine lovers. They also assist in bringing colour and spectacle to the celebrations for St. Vincent, the patron saint of French wine growers.

On the first Saturday following January 22nd (St. Vincent's Day), the Chevaliers du Tastevin visit a selected village in the Côte d'Or (a different one each year) to celebrate the health and continued good fortune of the vine with a procession and solemn mass.

COUSINERIE DE BOURGOGNE

Savigny-lès-Beaune is the home of the Cousinerie, whose aim is to promote the wines of this village slightly more than others. Since 1960, the Cousinerie has gained the reputation for hospitality and unswerving devotion to the pleasant task of putting Savigny-lès-Beaune on the map. They appear to undertake this duty with hilarity and considerable drawing of corks! Their activities include promotional dinners, tastings and organised visits in the region.

LES PILIERS CHABLISIENS

The purpose of the Chablis brotherhood is to announce twice a year the fame of their wines, and this is undertaken with great zeal. The major event takes place at the end of November, with a complete tasting of all the wines and subsequent overladen banquets. The brotherhood is based in 'Chablis, Yonne,

COMITÉ DE BOURGOGNE ET L'ORDRE DES GRANDS DUCS D'OCCIDENT

The activities of the Comité* are more specially devoted to the arts of Burgundy, but they do sponsor the Fête de la Vigne et du Vin, at the beginning of September in Dijon. Their centre is the magnificent twelfth-century cellar of Clairvaus, built by the monks of the Abbey of Clairvaux to store their wines.

Les Trois Glorieuses

This is the biggest Burgundian party of the year, and it brings together all the elements of the wine trade and the wine trade of the world: growers, brokers, *négociants,* merchants, buyers for huge concerns, those from independent and often smallish firms, hotel and restaurant chains and those who pride themselves on the wine lists of their catering establishments. Indeed, it is almost a pity to write about it because, unless you already have an invitation from someone in the wine trade who can assure you of accommodation, there will be no hope that you can find a room in which to stay, even within a hundred miles of Beaune. All hotel rooms are booked from year to year by the wine trade, private houses stuff visitors into their guest rooms, the shops in Beaune display all the gastronomic specialities—and, it is said, the police have instructions that they are not to apprehend any people revelling in the streets, but should guide them gently to wherever they may rest.

The Trois Glorieuses are held in the third weekend in November. On the Saturday, the cellars of the Hospices de Beaune are open for those who wish to taste—from the cask—the wines of the current vintage that are to be auctioned the next day. Huge crowds push their way in, many with *tastevin* in hand, but it is a job to get near the casks and often impossible to avoid spitting the young wine onto the floor without hitting someone's foot. On this day other tastings are held in Beaune, including a range of young Beaujolais in the Town Hall, and many of the great establishments hold special tastings in their cellars, some of them charging a small entrance fee, and many offering visitors the chance to try bottled wines of previous years, including really old Burgundies.

On the Saturday night, the Chevaliers du Tastevin (see page 6) hold a banquet at Clos de Vougeot. This, floodlit for the occasion, is also an occasion for honouring various visitors by admitting them into the Burgundian wine order, and some celebrity, such as an ambassador or other important personage, heads the list of those inducted. The meal is heralded by fanfares on the hunting horns traditional in France, sounded in the courtyard, and the proceedings, in addition to the inductions, are enlivened by the 'Cadets de Bourgogne' a group of

* Enquiries to: Cellier de Clairvaux, Boulevard de la Trémouille, 21 Dijon.

singers who are kept going throughout the many hours of the meal by draughts of wine. At intervals the whole company is invited to join in by singing the *Ban Bourguignon*, a song that consists chiefly of the syllables 'la, la la', with wagging of the hands held above the head and clappings.

On the Sunday afternoon, the auction of the Hospices wines is held—and for once the elaborate luncheons are cut short as hosts and buyers rush off to see the start of the sale.

Until 1959, the auction was actually held in the cellars of the Hospices, but in that year, the centenary, it was decided to hold the sale in a specially erected building in the market place. The occasion is social and exciting: television cameras, the press on the platform behind the auctioneers, and the auctioneer himself refreshed in what can be a six- or even eight-hour stint by a bottle of Meursault, under his table. The closing of the bidding is done '*a la chandelle*' that is, as a taper burns out. But, in this instance, there are two tapers, in a special holder; and the announcement '*Deuxieme Feu*' (second light) speeds up the bids, gathered from the Auctioneer's assistants, who parade throughout the hall. As long as a taper burns, the bidding continues. At the end of the sale of the wines, the marcs (page 34) and brandies are sold.

Eventually another banquet is held in the evening—often much delayed, if the sale is a long one and the auctioneer has to stay—and this takes place in the two cellars underneath the huge town wall and bastions. The food is prepared and served by the students of the hotel schools in the vicinity, and is both elaborate and elaborately presented—even though several hundred have to be coped with in a confined space.

In years that are definitely 'off' for the wines, the auction is not held, and the wines that can be offered for sale are sold privately. It is sometimes said that the prices that are paid are artificially high, because of the buyers being compelled to go on bidding, on account of this being, in the words of some journalists, "the biggest charity sale in the world". The fact that the wines are from the Côte de Beaune, too, means that they cannot be representative of the finest reds of Burgundy. But it is also fair to say that the sale does attract invaluable publicity to Burgundy, and that buyers from all over the world can meet, discuss not merely the current vintage but others with their *négociants* and friends, and that the sort of prices that are paid—which make headlines in the French papers and achieve space in many others—do indicate the general level that good Burgundy has achieved in a particular year.

On the Monday of the weekend, the strong-willed move on to Meursault, for the lunch known as 'La Paulée'. This word is the local one for the vintage lunch given by vineyard proprietors to their workers; in the mid 1930s (the time of world depression, which nevertheless saw the recreation of the wine order, the Chevaliers du Tastevin, as a publicity effort), the Mayor of Meursault decided that, to publicise the great wines of Burgundy, he would enlarge the local practice. So now the Town Hall of Meursault is given over to about 300 growers, shippers, vineyard workers, and such visitors as can be squeezed in (once in, it is physically impossible to get out). All bring their finest bottles, for sharing around the tables. It is a matter of pride that each proprietor or grower should have something really special to show off to his neighbours, and the exchanging of bottles is a very happy, heart-warming gesture. Though there may be some 'personality' who is the chief guest at the lunch, who may speak in reply to a tribute paid, it is an occasion of informality and robust cheer.

Wine and Gastronomic Fairs

A list of wine and gastronomic fairs might assist in the planning of a Burgundy journey, though a warning needs to be offered—beware of great crowds and long tastings of average wines. That said, it can be great fun in a totally lighthearted way, and provide an insight into French selling methods.

La Foire Nationale des Vins. Held at Mâcon (Saône-et-Loire) during the spring (the date varies from year to year). Enquiries should be addressed to the Chambre du Commerce at Mâcon. While the Fair offers wines from most regions, there is a wide selection of Burgundy, which can show quickly the differences between areas' and growers' wines.

La Foire aux Vins de Table. Held in the middle of August at Chagny, a quiet town just off the old main road N6 and close to the last southern villages of the Côte de Beaune, this fair gives an opportunity to taste all the generic *appellations* of red and white Burgundy. An entrance fee is charged, plus tasting tickets.

L'Exposition Générale des Vins de Bourgogne. This is a well-organised two-day tasting held just before the sale by auction of the wines of the Hospices de Beaune during the third weekend of November. It is a mainly trade affair where the young wines are on show alongside older vintages. Entrance can be arranged by contacting: Le Secrétariat des Association Viticoles, 20 Place Monge, Beaune (Côte d'Or).

Foire Gastronomique. Held in the first two weeks of November in Dijon, it has won a reputation for an amazing and tantalising range of gastronomic delights with a fair selection of Burgundy wines for sampling. Though a trade fair in origin, it has been opened to the public on payment of an entrance fee. Enquiries: Boîte Postale 122, Dijon (Côte d'Or).

La Fête Raclet. On the last weekend of October, this fair is held in the Beaujolais and is named after Bernard Raclet, who discovered a treatment against the *pyralis* grub which affected the vineyards in the late 1830s. The Fête is the first opportunity for the trade to taste a whole range of Beaujolais Nouveaux. To enjoy the festivities to the full, one needs to be in the company of a member of the Burgundy wine trade.

2
The History

The hill formation of the ridge that is today known as the Côte d'Or, the heart of the Burgundy wine country, was created during the Jurassic period, 150 million years ago. Archaeologists have found traces of man living there 12,000 years B.C., when horses were driven up and off the rock of Solutré to perish on the cliffs below and serve as fodder for humans. Works of art dating from the sixth century B.C. were found in 1952 at Châtillon-sur-Seine, and, in the Bronze Age, what is now part of Burgundy was crossed by trading tracks that made it known as 'the highway of tin and amber'.

Caesar conquered Gaul and what were the tribes of the region of Burgundy in 52 B.C. and, subsequently, Roman civilisation extended widely in the area. The actual name 'Burgundia' is first noted about A.D. 500, and refers to fair-skinned warriors from Germany who took over the region. In the latter part of the fourth century, the Franks and the Burgundians had become Christian. At this time the area belonged to France. Later, in the eighth century under Charlemagne (who interested himself seriously in wine growing), it became increasingly prosperous, due to the richness of the land as well as its strategic importance. One of Charlemagne's ordinances forbade the treading of grapes by foot as, even then it was considered unhygienic. His name is remembered over the centuries for his vineyard holdings in Corton, and commemorated in the white wine of the Corton Charlemagne. However, after Charlemagne's death in 814 the region was divided, and Burgundy became a duchy at the beginning of the eleventh century.

The Middle Ages

Burgundy was of enormous importance in the Middle Ages, both because of its powerful dukes and on account of the growth of the power of the religious orders in the region. As early as the sixth century there is a record of a piece of land in the Dijon region being donated by the then King of Burgundy,

Gontram, in the form of the Abbey of St. Benigne. From this time onwards families granted the status of nobles made many gifts to the church of vineyards or properties where vines could be cultivated. In addition, many nobles themselves owned wine-producing estates. The dominating influence in the evolution of Burgundy wine, however, was certainly the church. The great churches and abbeys of Burgundy are witness to the prosperity and importance of the religious orders. The mighty foundation of Cluny, established in the tenth century by a pious Duke of Aquitaine, was so powerful that its abbot often exercised more authority even than the pope. The Cluniac monks acted through their daughter abbeys as, in Sir Stephen Runciman's words, "the American Express of the Middle Ages". They ran hostels for pilgrims and travellers, pursued scholarly research of all kinds, copied and illuminated texts, acted as teachers and doctors, as well as being possibly the supreme exponents of the sacred liturgy.

In 1098, three Cluniac monks, including an Englishman, Stephen Hardy, set up a separate establishment at Cîteaux—so called because it was in a low-lying, marshy place, among the reeds, *cistels.* Here they revived the austerity and discipline of earlier monastic traditions. St. Bernard, who preached the Third Crusade in Burgundy, came to Cîteaux in 1112 and encouraged this reforming spirit by founding the Abbey of Clairvaux. In addition, the Cistercians became renowned as wine producers, showing how poor soil, fit for nothing else, could be cultivated to produce remarkable wine. They established a branch of their order at what is now Clos de Vougeot—its shape and style are typically Cistercian—and in 1141 the nuns of the Cistercian Abbey of Notre Dame du Tart purchased a vineyard in Morey, which remained in their possession until the French Revolution. This vineyard, the world-famous Clos de Tart, has never been split up between owners and now belongs in its entirety to the well-known shipper Mommessin, of Mâcon.

Golden Age

The 'Golden Age' of the Duchy of Burgundy was the fourteenth century, after Philippe le Hardi, fourth son of the King of France, became Duke of Burgundy on the death of his father. He was succeeded by Jeans Sans Peur, Philippe le Bon, and Charles le Téméraire; and the period between 1364 and 1477 was brilliant as regards works of art, economic and political achievements and extravagantly lavish entertainments and social life. The Duchy was enormously powerful, its Dukes ruling the entire Netherlands, Artois, Picardy, Luxembourg and the Franche-Comté in addition to Burgundy itself. Even the King of France was in awe of the Duke of Burgundy, whose forces were of prime importance in any war. The French court drank the wines of Burgundy, both for reasons of diplomacy and of proximity. Philippe le Bon, on his marriage to Isabella of Portugal in 1429, created the chivalric order of the Golden Fleece, one of the most influential brotherhoods of its kind, which still exists to this day. In 1430, at a banquet in honour of the new duchess, a gigantic pie was presented; this held a giant and a live sheep, its fleece painted blue and its horns gold. Accounts of the ducal catering are extraordinary: the 'chief pantler' or steward had fifty esquires under him just to serve the meals. Go into the courtyard of the Hospices de Beaune and appreciate the wealth that made it possible.

Burgundy was again joined to the French crown in the fifteenth century, but its boundaries were extended and its governors were still men of great importance, who, being concerned with protecting the Duchy's frontiers, were in a position to maintain a type of independence, which lasted until the outbreak of the French Revolution. The Austrians invaded Burgundy and occupied it after the Battle of Waterloo in 1815. In the Franco-Prussian War, the French were victorious at the Battle of Nuits in 1870 and at Dijon in 1871; this is why the Cross of the Légion d'Honneur is seen in the arms of Dijon.

War—and Peace

In World War II, Burgundy had to endure the advance of the Allied forces from the south and the pulling out of the Germans; great tales are told of how stocks of fine wines were hidden so as not to be looted. One would-be clever producer sank his in a pond—but to his horror the labels came unstuck and floated off, so that the Germans were able to recover the bottles. Wynford Vaughan Thomas, a liaison officer between the British, American and French forces, related how the French general in command had halted just below Beaune, in a dilemma as to whether his duty really impelled him to launch his troops over what were the finest slopes of the Côte; the British and Americans couldn't understand his delaying. All at H.Q. were sunk in doubt and despair when suddenly a motor-cyclist arrived breathless and flung himself into the C.O.'s presence with a cry—"Mon Général, the Germans are only occupying the inferior slopes!" At which the general leapt to his feet with a roar of "J'attaque!"

The attraction of Burgundy probably lies in the fact that it is essentially a country region, even its largest towns never wholly cutting one off from the winding lanes, fat pastures and dumpy grey stone houses among fields, plantations of trees and, never far away, vineyards. It is a countryman's country and its wines are the wines of those who have a direct and wholehearted ability to enjoy life. Little wonder that so many of us love it so much!

3
How Burgundy is Made

The method of winemaking in Burgundy has always been a keen topic of conversation, both within the region and amongst the export trade. Discussion of how Burgundy is made—or how it should be made—is lively, much more so than in the other great wine regions, because 'fashion', a high-sounding word of economic requirements, has often decided the growers as to the style of wine to make. They are not, in making wine, producing a fine product without any reference to what their customers want. They have to sell the wine once it is made.

Even though the laws of *Appellation Contrôlée* fix the grape varieties to be used, determine the quantities permitted, and decide many other factors of winegrowing, it is still quite possible for the Burgundy grower to be individual in his methods of vinification, thus causing a wide variety of wine 'personalities' to be created from the basic ingredients at the disposal of all.

Varieties of Grapes

The grape varieties used for red wines are: 'Pinot Noir' (used for all the Côte d'Or and Côte Chalonnaise wines); and 'Gamay' (the Beaujolais grape, which is also grown in outlying areas of the Côte d'Or and is often blended with 'Pinot Noir' for the label *Passe Tout Grains*—see page 114).

For white wines, there are: 'Chardonnay' (used for all the white wines from the Côte d'Or, Côte Chalonnaise and Chablis, which are to qualify for vineyard, village and area appellations—see page 114); and 'Aligoté', which is sold under the grape variety name, and is not a regional appellation.

PINOT NOIR

If you walk into the vineyards during July, August and September, the ripening bunches of Pinot Noir grapes are closer knit and smaller in size than you would expect by comparison with other wine grapes. This tight bunching can cause rot during either wet or humid weather, and is only made up for by the elegance and finesse of the Pinot Noir wines, now long established as the only grape variety for red wines capable of maintaining this fine concentration of flavour to the exclusion of all other varieties.

As fine wines rarely appear in abundance, so with the production capabilities of the Pinot Noir. It gives a relatively modest yield from the great villages of the Côte de Nuits and Côte de Beaune, where the permitted quantity level vintaged is 35 hectolitres per hectare (this permitted yield is called the '*rendement*'). Increases can be applied for and granted in particularly fruitful years, although this takes place usually in vintages where, for natural reasons, the quantity anyway exceeds the permitted level dramatically, and the character of the wine is light and fast maturing (see page 113 on A. C.). This 35 hectolitres per hectare is equivalent in normal bottle terms to 4,655 bottles per hectare, which clearly indicates the small production of estates or domaines of only a few hectares each (another reason why fine Burgundy is seldom abundant!) In Burgundy both growers and *négotiatiants* count sales per bottle—and not in cases of a dozen bottles.

The quantity of wine from the Pinot Noir will also be affected by the average age of the vines within the vineyard. Though it is quite normal to find vineyards where the vines are all one age, one cannot say this is altogether good husbandry. For, when replanting eventually takes place, the juice of the young vines cannot be used for *appellation* wines until after the third year of the vines' life; the most satisfactory practice is to keep replanting on a regular and continuous basis, so as to maintain the essential balance of the vineyard's yield. Vines will live up to forty years, even, exceptionally, reaching sixty or seventy years. The oldest vines must be in Vosne Romanée—one hectare over ninety years old. Note, when you look at a vineyard, how the older vines are thicker in their trunks and considerably gnarled. They produce fewer grapes as they age, but make fine wine.

After uprooting, vineyards should be allowed at least one year to lie fallow. These fallow areas can be easily noticed on the slopes by the telltale strips of bare land.

The juice of the Pinot Noir is without colour, and the same black grape variety is used in the production of Champagne. If you dare to pinch a ripening Pinot Noir, do not expect a mouthful of sweetness—the bitterness will dry your tongue. Indeed, very few fine wine grapes are pleasant to eat.

GAMAY

This is a world-famous wine grape, named after the village of Gamay, which is on the RN6, next to Saint Aubin. Planted in the Côte d'Or, it can only be used to help make the blend with 'Pinot Noir' for the label *Passe Tout Grains* (this must consist of two-thirds 'Gamay' with one-third 'Pinot Noir'). The 'Gamay' is the wonderful grape that produces the fresh, fruity

Beaujolais where the soil and sharply undulating countryside bring out the very best that this variety can do. It yields well in many vineyards throughout the world but, in the Côte d'Or region, the idea of quality from the 'Gamay' has, historically, been much despised. Remember that no 'Gamay' wine can produce a Côte d'Or or Côte Chalonnaise wine bearing a vineyard, village or area label.

CHARDONNAY

This is the noble white grape of all Burgundy. The 'Chardonnay' is responsible for the finest dry white wines in the world; they range in style from the roundness of Meursault, the lighter more aggressive Pouilly Fuissé, the chalky dryness of Chablis and back again to the unique maturity of smells and tonal flavours of the sublime Montrachets.

With the possibility of greatness being so close, the 'Chardonnay' is demanding in the way it is cultivated. The same quantities per hectare are allowed as for the 'Pinot Noir', but, in the initial stages of winemaking, the fermentation of 'Chardonnay' wines takes much longer than for reds (see page 30).

In the vineyards of villages where both red and white wines are produced (such as Chassagne Montrachet), it will be impossible for the beginner in wine to pick out the 'Chardonnay' vines from those of the 'Pinot Noir' until the ripening has begun to colour the grapes from July until vintage time. So do not be put off if the difference between the two grape varieties is not apparent to the eye. When the grape variety colour does reveal itself, during the high summer, ownership of the land is so diffuse that red and white grapes are often side by side. The vines are planted one metre apart and grow one metre high.

As with the 'Pinot Noir', the 'Chardonnay' grape is used world-wide in an attempt to reproduce the fine qualities traditionally available from the historic Côte d'Or vineyards.

While no direct similarity can be acknowledged, the determined efforts of the growers in California to copy the true Burgundies by adopting the two noble grape varieties cannot be ignored. A few of the best qualities of Californian wine have now reached European standards and will be sustained by an ambitious programme of improvement. Personally, I am not in favour of wines being labelled according to their grape variety only ('varietal' is the U.S. term, 'cultivar' the South African). I believe these terms are misleading and confusing, though obviously the intention is the exact opposite. Grapes are too strongly influenced by soil, weather and vinification to be marketed under varietal labels—unless the object in time is gradually to produce a uniform quality, lacking in individuality. Surely, area or shippers' names should mean more to drinkers of fine wines than the grape variety? Unless care is shown, the international wine drinker risks believing that a

'Chardonnay' from the Napa valley will taste the same as a 'Chardonnay' from the Mâconnais!

ALIGOTÉ

This is a white grape used wholly for white wines, which are slightly sharp and dry in taste. The 'Aligoté' is grown in varying quantities throughout the Burgundy region and the wines are sold at a modest price in shops and restaurants. They are always sold while young, for the hallmark of 'Aligoté is the freshness and cleansing acidity. Being a cheap wine from a great area, there is a real threat to future production, as many 'Aligoté' vineyards are being replanted with 'Chardonnay—which, according to the vineyards' position, may also entitle their wines to a higher and more valuable *appellation*, and command a higher price for the grower. While Bourgogne 'Aligoté' is sold only under the generic title, if you see a grower's bottling using this grape it will probably indicate (by the name of his village) which area is responsible for the wine. Favoured sites for 'Aligoté' in the Côte d'Or are the higher slopes—as the vine is hardy—and it is worth particularly mentioning the villages of Pernand Vergelesses, next to Corton, Savigny-lès-Beaune, and the region of Mercurey in the Côte Chalonnaise.

A very worthwhile drive is provided by the road through Pernand Vergelesses up into the wild country behind the Bois de Corton, following the signs to Nuits St. Georges. En route there is an excellent 'Aligoté resort' at the Caveau de Dégustation at Marey-lès-Fussey. Up on this plateau, vineyards are well above the normal altitude recommended for the vine's comfort, but today's improved technology has given the growers fresh heart and their efforts have had splendid results, especially for the Aligoté. A Burgundian lunch can be taken at the Caveau and parties can be catered for if prior warning is given.

An alternative fruit to the grape up on the plateau is *cassis* (blackcurrant), and it is the 'Aligoté' wine which, blended with the *cassis* liqueur, makes the Burgundian apéritif *vin blanc cassis* or *Kir* (see page 33). This will conquer all tiredness and any palate jaded by too much Burgundian food and wine.

Bourgogne 'Aligoté' has never been easy to sell in the U.K., and one suspects that, in the bad old days, it was occasionally used as a blending wine for bulk shipments. An interesting tasting would be to observe the difference in style and character of the 'Aligoté' by comparing 'Aligoté' wines from the Chablis (quite chalky), the Côte d'Or (firm and fatter) and the Côte Chalonnaise (with higher acidity and 'greener'). Personally, I favour the 'Aligoté' of Chablis the most for straight drinking, and the Chalonnaise 'Aligoté' for the *vin blanc cassis* blend.

The Vineyard Cycle

Some knowledge of what is involved with the cultivation of the vine month by month throughout the year can help the reader to gain a general idea of the annual cycle of events that produce Burgundy. It isn't just picking grapes in the autumn! At weekends and even late into the evening, those who own small plots will go to work outside the hours of their own regular jobs. If you see people in the vineyards this is what they may be doing in different months, whether they are self-employed or working for an owner. Some of the tasks on which they are engaged may be routine, others require skill and experience. Women and even quite small children will take part—and, even though the work is hard, it is a dedicated routine, often carried on in extremes of wet and cold as well as in the heat of summer. It is back-breaking, too, because the vines are pruned low, so that anyone expecting to earn an easy payment of holiday picking is destined to find out the hard way—by spending hours doubled up so as to get at the grapes.

The curious double-bellied baskets, used only in Burgundy for gathering grapes, are extremely heavy to carry when full.

VINEYARD CALENDAR

January. The vines are pruned. Skill is needed in judging where the pruning should be done, so that the branches of the plant may be trained along the wires that support them during the exuberant period of flowering and then while the grapes are developing. If the branches are too short, the grapes will not be abundant. If they are too long, they may sag to the ground, risking the embryo grapes becoming chilled in the spring frosts or, later, getting rotten by being in contact with the earth. The system of pruning in the Côte d'Or is known as the '*Cordon Guyot*' and consists of training the principal branch along a wire roughly one foot above the soil, then a double wire above that for the shoots and then a further wire higher still to accommodate the full vine growth of a metre high. This enables the vines to enjoy maximum exposure to the sun and air, without risking getting battered by rain or, worse, hail, and being too heated by the sun later in the year.

February. Pruning goes on and should be finished in this month. The weather often hampers work outside, but this is a time when equipment of various types is prepared.

March. The soil that was placed protectively around the vines to shield them from frost and possible snow in the winter is now raked away, so that they are able to receive the benefit of the sun and air. A special type of tractor is used to aerate the earth in the vineyard or, if the plot is small, this is done by hand. When a vineyard has been replanted, this is the time when the young vines are grafted on to disease-resistant root stock.

April. The vineyard is generally tidied up now that spring is coming. The prunings and trimmings of the vines are burned and the wires are fixed along which the tendrils of the vine will be supported. The young vines are planted.

May. There is still a danger of frost. The 'Ice Saints' (SS. Pancratius, Servatius, Boniface and Sophie) whose festivals are celebrated in mid-May represent a critical period, hence their name. A frost now can prevent the flower of the vine forming. So small heating pots and other warming devices appear in vineyards as safeguards. At the same time, weeds are removed—either by ploughing or else by hand—since they would take the nourishment from the vines. The vines are also probably sprayed against various diseases, especially mildew, with copper sulphate solution that turns their leaves bluish in colour. Nowadays many highly mechanised devices do this spraying, but you may also see men with a spray carried on their back, directing the nozzle of the spray with their hand.

June. In this month the vine should flower—tiny flowers that nevertheless give a pungent scent to the vineyard when they open. Ideally, the flowering should take place within a short time and not be interfered with by rain or cold weather. The best shoots of the vine are now attached to the wires and any that are superfluous are cut away. Spraying probably goes on.

July. The vineyard may be ploughed again—it is getting warm and the aeration is necessary. Weeds must also continue to be removed, unwanted shoots cut off and spraying continued.

August. Many people in France are on holiday during this month, but the wine-maker will be getting his cellar ready for the vintage. Vats and casks must be cleaned and prepared and machinery checked and put in order. Weeding must go on in the vineyard. By now, the black grapes will begin to turn from yellowish-green to an increasingly dark purple.

September. The white grapes swell and become an almost luminous greenish-yellow. The black grapes fill out. This is vintage month and picking usually starts in about the third week. If weather permits, the grapes are gathered as they are judged to be ripe but not overripe, and are taken to the cellar to be crushed and the juice allowed to begin the process of fermentation. Pickers who are self-employed usually work all the hours of daylight, in a favourable season, while they have need to do so, other bands of pickers work to a more regular routine, but a vintage day is invariably long.

October. The vintage goes on into at least the first and second weeks. After it has finished, the vineyard is fertilised and any new plantations that may have previously been lying fallow are now prepared for planting by deep ploughing. In the cellars, the process of finishing and appraising the new wine goes on.

November. Soil is raked over the vine roots to protect them during the winter. Non-productive shoots and dead twigs are pruned for kindling wood. Sometimes the shoots and twigs will be burnt in the vineyard, showing spirals of light grey smoke against the wintry background.

December. The November tasks are continued in the vineyard and in the cellars the wine-making equipment is cleaned and put away, while the new wine continues to 'make itself'.

Filling the vat (cuve) with grapes during the harvest

We can start the story of how Burgundy wines are made in February, when vineyard work begins again. The winter months are spent by the growers working in the cellar, watching over the new wine from the previous vintage and preparing the older wines for bottling in the spring.

There are no precise bottling dates, as these decisions are entirely left to the grower or shipper, but for red wines it would be quite normal for a grower to have three vintages in his cellar in February—the new wine, and the wines of the previous two vintages. However, earlier bottling of Burgundy has found some new advocates today, and maturation in wood has been shortened by many growers, so as to release their wine for sale at an earlier date. Every month that a wine, either in wood or in bottle, occupies space in a cellar costs money for its keep. This is often forgotten by the drinker. It should be remembered that the local wine market in Burgundy or, for that matter, in the wine regions of France, is accustomed to drinking relatively fine wines much younger than the customers of the export trade.

During February and March there will be plenty of cellar activity in preparing export orders ready for despatch after the worst winter cold is over. No fine wines should be shipped in the extreme cold or even the heat of the high summer. They may suffer seriously if they travel then. While writing this chapter, I heard of a container of a thousand cases of excellent Burgundy being offloaded on to the dockside of New York and simply left outside over a weekend. It was a disaster—for all the white wines threw a crystal sediment as a result of being chilled so brutally. This does not necessarily affect the flavour at all, but the U.S. market hates deposits or sediment in bottles, suspecting their presence as somehow indicative of a faulty wine (an error, but the U.S. buyer wants only 'star bright' wines).

PRUNING

In the vineyard in the middle of February, the grower must organise the first pruning of the vines, and this is a task involving care and detailed attention. The purpose of pruning is to control the future growth of the vine and eliminate unwanted shoots. In this work, the laws of A.C. governing the method of pruning must be observed. For the Côte d'Or the '*taille guyot*' is the adopted pruning style. It can be described briefly: The main branch of the vine (*la baguette*) is trained along a wire some 30 cm from the ground. Above that is a double wire, to which the shoots of the main branch are tied and, to complete the trellis effect, a further single wire runs along the top. These wires are held taut by embedded wooden posts.

Each year the vine is pruned to retain two branches, the *baguette* as mentioned, and another, the *caisson*, which is the replacement branch for the following year. Just occasionally you will see an experimental pruning method—'*taille haute*'—where the vines are trained higher off the ground, according to the theory that they thus more easily escape late spring ground frosts and excessive summer heat. In Alsace and Germany this method has been successful, but so far it is too new in Burgundy to know whether permission will be granted or even recommended for its use with the better quality wines.

During the spring, when the chance of frost has virtually disappeared, the earth-covered vine roots are cleared to allow the young shoots to receive a circulation of fresh air. Then they will sprout healthily in April.

There has been an experiment at the Domaine St. Michel in Santenay, where plastic sheeting was used to cover the roots of young vines. Apparently great success in protection has been gained, although the wind causes a flapping of the sheets and a hideous high-pitched whistle hits the ears.

POTENTIAL HAZARDS

Before taking the winemaking procedure further, some of the potential hazards to which the vine is exposed will help to illustrate the constant battle the vineyard proprietor wages.

Frost. If spring temperatures fall below freezing (as low as 25°F or −4°C), the vine is likely to suffer a diminution of eventual yield. If a grower thinks late spring frosts are likely, he will delay pruning and will wait until 15th May before the danger is considered past. This period—known in the wine world as that of the 'Ice Saints', because the feasts of SS. Pancratius, Servatius, Boniface and Sophia occur then—is an important one. Once it is safely over, vintage prospects are hopeful.

Hail. This can cause local but cruel damage. In some regions noted for their exposure, the risk is sufficiently great for experiments in cloud dispersal by aeroplane to have been tried—though no one reports much success to date. Hail, battering the stems of the vine and leaving permanent traces, weakens it and destroys the vegetation. I have seen a vineyard at Chassagne Montrachet lose 30% of its possible quantity in one day in June 1974. If the grapes are already formed, hail can split and destroy them. The flavour of an otherwise successful wine can also be subtly and adversely affected by hail.

Coulure. This is when the partly formed grapes drop, rotting, from the vine. *Coulure* is transmitted by virus disease or infected grafting. It results usually from wet and cold weather at the vine's flowering time in June, with subsequent destruction of flowers and small berries. The white grape, 'Chardonnay', is more susceptible than the red 'Pinot Noir' to *coulure,* although the treatment is the same. One must remove the infected vine, disinfect the soil and replant a young, healthy vine.

Millerandage. A result of slight *coulure,* when bunches of grapes do not fully ripen, *millerandage* leaves only small green berries on the vine. If these bunches reach the winemaking stage, they impart a harsh and bitter flavour to the wine.

Oïdium. Also known as 'downy mildew', *oïdium* is a fungus disease, appearing during warm, humid weather. The vine leaves and grapes will be spoilt by black stains and small, unpleasant moulds during June and July. Preventive vine-spraying with sulphur is therefore an essential job during the early summer before the flowering, and again before the *véraison* (the time when the black grapes start to turn red from their original colour of white). If *oïdium* is detected early, it may not be necessary to dig up the vine, as there are now strong disinfectant sprays available to deal with it.

Mildew. This is another fungus disease which occur during humid weather. If it is allowed to develop, the leaves will fall;

the berries lose their food lifeline and, should any infected grapes be harvested with healthy grapes, the resulting wine will have an acrid taste and lack colour.

The treatment of mildew involves spraying with Bordeaux mixture, a copper sulphate and dissolved lime solution. Helicopters have been introduced for spraying at speed and they are amazingly accurate, aided by the coloured discs seen standing in the vineyards as markers of the vine rows.

SUMMER IN THE VINEYARD

The vineyard calendar takes a major step forward in early June, when the grower will anxiously await a healthy *fleuraison*—the flowering of the vine. These flowers are not spectacular, indeed, they have to be looked for by the untrained eye and seem merely tiny flowers on the vine shoot. But they are most attractive in their smell, being fragrant and slightly musky. On a still day, at early evening, a walk through the vines, particularly uphill, can be a conscious stroll through scent. The delicate fragrance is elusive but, once experienced, never forgotten.

During this time, spraying by hand, tractor or helicopter is a major activity, and the growers watch carefully for signs of vine disease, and observe the progress of each plot.

By July and August, the vines should be growing rapidly, following the training on wires established during the pruning. If the growth at vinetop level becomes too abundant, there is a lopping to clear the way through to the grapes for the sun's rays and to concentrate the feeding process into the grapes, not into unwanted leaves.

As the vintage takes place traditionally a hundred days after the flowering, this high summer period can be seen as vital with regard to balanced weather conditions. Hours of sunshine, some gentle rain, a few days, low humidity, no hail and no storms—that is the ideal. These climatic conditions cannot be helped by man, as the laws of A.C. do not permit irrigation, even in hot summers lacking rain. Thus nature takes the major part in deciding the quality of a vintage. Fortunately, in Burgundy, it rarely lets the grower down; with improved viticultural knowledge, the number of years hitting low points became fewer. To date, 1968 was the last real disaster.

When September arrives, the vintage is only a few weeks away, by which time all the preparations to receive the harvest must be completed. The fermentation oak vats are thoroughly cleaned and scrubbed; the *paniers* (grape pickers' baskets) are brought out and repaired; the grape presses are checked for working order. Cellars are cleaned and tidied, and those on holiday return for the high spot of the vineyard year.

VINTAGE TIME

The next decision the grower will face is the date of picking the grapes (the vintage or *vendange*). Science can assist him by providing an analysis of the juice of sample grape bunches, which can now be analysed from day to day or even hour to hour, but the weather remains the greatest factor in determining the quality of the crop.

In recent Burgundy vintages, there have been several fine summers with an inevitable anticipation of great vintages, which have been spoilt or altered by heavy rain coming at vintage time. Rain will increase the quantity of wine by swelling the grapes, but the loss of quality will be noticeable by the lack of body in the wine. Will the grower start when the grapes are ready early? Or will he wait, in the hope of continued sunshine

Traditional hand press

to improve the grapes further—and risk rain spoiling the crop? Whatever the decision, vintaging usually starts between 20th September and 19th October.

In the Burgundy region, vineyard holdings are small and for the picking friends and families join together, leaving little need for much outside labour to be imported for the tiring, backbreaking work so close to the ground. Everyone who can picks, the oddly shaped double baskets peculiar to the region then receiving the contents of individual *paniers* or trugs. The *paniers Beaunois*, suspended on poles, are very heavy when full.

The stronger *vendageurs* (pickers) get the job of lifting the full *panier* on to the transport for delivery to the presshouse. At this point the A.C. laws demand a certificate for each travelling load of grapes, thereby beginning the control and record of quantity of the wine. The majority of all growers in the Côte d'Or vinify their grapes themselves (other wine regions noted for quantity and less historical fame use a co-operative system extensively and successfully for vinification). In very abundant years, some grapes are sold to the *négociants* so that the shippers make the wine. But the sale of grapes in Burgundy by the grower to the shipper is a declining practice today.

When the grapes arrive at the presshouse, they will be analysed again for sugar and acidity content, giving the information necessary for judging if chaptalisation is needed. Knowledge of the future alcoholic strength is important if the wine wants to claim an A.C.

Chaptalisation is a widely used practice in Burgundy to bolster wines which are likely to have insufficient natural sugar in the grape must (*moût*)—the juice before it becomes wine. The wine yeasts feed on the sugar and cannot work satisfactorily if there is not enough. Growers are permitted to add up to a maximum of 200 kilos of sugar per hectare of vines during fermentation: they must not, by this method, increase the eventual alcoholic strength of the wine by more than 2°. This long-established addition of sugar must not be overdone, as its object is to balance the many complex constituents of the wine more successfully than nature has done. Over-chaptalised wines will be heavy and unnatural in taste, giving way later to a blandness of flavour, but most chaptalised wines will not be remarked on for this introduction of sugar. Done with skill, it should in no way make the wine obviously sweet or treacly.

Ideally, grapes will be pressed immediately they arrive at the *fouloirégrappoir* (a cylindrical press that crushes the grapes, but not the pips, and strips the berries off the stalks). The old wooden press, turned by hand, is a romantic antique today.

The juice and pulp from the crushing is pumped to the oak fermentation vats; some growers and more shippers have purchased enamel-lined vats, which are easier to keep clean —for at this stage, the young wine is susceptible to infection.

The manner in which the grower carries on the vinification will determine the character and quality of the resulting wine. Obviously, this is the point at which the differences in making red and white wines become apparent, but before showing these differences, a short restatement of the what and how of fermentation may give some understanding of the vintner's art.

FERMENTATION

Before the experiments of Louis Pasteur in the mid-1850s, the chemical process of fermentation was little understood and only his work defined the actual conversion of the natural sugar in the juice and must into carbon dioxide and alcohol. The agent for this conversion is the 'bloom' on the skin of the ripe grape, which contains the yeast/enzymes (*Saccharomyces cerevisiae*). Most of the chemical constituents present in the must remain after fermentation, though the sugars are greatly reduced and alcohol, with esters and some new acids, appears.

In practice, the juice and pulp will be pumped from the press into the traditional oak vats or, today, tanks. These are not filled to the top as the fermentation process is violent enough to overflow the vat when in full action.

Red Wines

Once the fermentation vat is filled to the correct height, it will depend, usually, on the temperature as to whether the fermentation begins immediately. Between 22°C and 30°C (72°F and 86°F) is the natural range of temperatures for fermentation.

If the weather is cold and the fermentation is reluctant to start, then the cellars will be heated to get everything going, for the yeasts cannot work if too cold or too hot. Control of temperature during fermentation is vital, and the growers will closely watch the temperature gauge. If it looks at all likely that the process is slowing down through cold, then they are prepared to help the process with the aid of hot water pipes round the cellar. Alternatively, if the must looks to be overheating, then cold water will be passed through the pipes or the cellar doors left open. It is during this part of the fermentation that analyses are taken to check future alcoholic strengths in case some sugar needs to be added to the must.

Red Burgundy is a fully fermented wine, with no residual sugar (sugar left in the finished wine). If you ever taste a Burgundy where there is a definite sweet flavour, then you may well worry about its provenance.

While fermentation takes place, the gas given off by the process escapes and the pulpy mush floats to the top of the vat (this is called the *chapeau* or hat). This crust is often broken up and pushed down again to immerse all the skins, pips and their constituents in the fermenting juice. The fermentation will end once the sugar is fully converted into alcohol. For red wines, six days on average will see the process complete.

ANCIENNE MÉTHODE

The expression '*méthode ancienne*' (old style vinification) became fashionable a few years ago, and was used to describe a style of fermentation when all the stalks were left in the must and the pulp was left in contact with the fermented juice for more than a fortnight. The purpose was to provide darker, fuller and more flavoured wines. However, '*méthode ancienne*' is a doubtful title, because Burgundian vinification reveals no definite historical references to this manner of winemaking. Traditionally, Burgundy wines were quickly fermented and the wine separated from the *marc* (pulp) after a few days.

Obviously, these fermentation decisions are entirely individual and the future wine must be judged on its merit. However, the slightly misleading term '*méthode ancienne*' is now less prominent in the commercial language of the Côte d'Or than it was a few years ago—I think for good reasons.

Maturation

Once the grower decides his wine has had sufficient contact with the *marc* (pulp), the wine is pumped off into oak casks (*pièces* is the Burgundy word) to recover and begin the next stage of its life.

Transferring wine from large storage vats to casks for further maturation and development

Wine undergoes a secondary fermentation, the malo-lactic, in which the malic acid is converted into lactic acid. In red Burgundy, this will take about six months of slow, more gentle fermentation, and is liable to stop and re-start without warning. Some gas is let off and, putting your ear to the *pièce*, you can hear this gentle bubbling. During this stage of its fermentation, the wine will be unclear and most difficult to taste. Indeed, you should not try to do so. If you ever taste a red Burgundy which has a fine bead of bubble around the wine's rim, which then imparts a prickle on the tongue, you have probably got a wine that was bottled before the malo-lactic fermentation was fully finished. This fault still occurs just a bit too often in

Burgundy, for the analysis can tell, with almost total accuracy, whether this secondary fermentation was finished or not.

Tasting before racking (changing the wine from one cask to another)

During this early maturation in wood, the grower will guard and nurture his wines with parental care. According to his judgment, several cellar tasks related to the new wine will be decided: the fining (*collage*) to clarify the wine; the racking (*soutirage*), moving the wine from one cask to another leaving behind the cask deposit or lees; the topping up of the cask (*ouillage*) after the natural loss by evaporation.

The length of time the wine remains in cask before bottling will be decided by the grower or the *négociant*. If the grower sells his wine in wood, it can be removed to the *négociant*'s cellar for his staff to take over the care of it, though in some cases the wine may change ownership yet remain with the grower for later transfer, prior to bottling.

BOTTLING

Whoever takes the decision to bottle, this is a major event in the life cycle of the wine. A fine and experienced palate alone will know when the correct time has arrived for the *mise en bouteilles*.

Growers tend to have fairly simple bottling methods—well-tried and traditional—although some cellars capable of making very fine wine create some anxiety for the health of their wine at bottling. Cleanliness and super hygiene are a necessity—look for it always. A cellar may look picturesque, but at bottling time it ought to look surgically clean.

Négociants, by the style of their business, undertake regular bottling programmes with expensive fixed equipment. Progress has been made in recent years in raising the standards of filtration and sterile bottling has become the accepted practice. When visiting cellars, it will be interesting to look out for the variety of equipment now required to maintain a shipper's business. Heavy sums in capital expenditure have been invested by the shippers, all of whom seek a high turnover of the cheaper wines to justify the cost of such installations. To an extent, the successful cheaper wines will help to finance the longer maturity dates of the fine wines. It is the cheaper wines that are required in quantity and it is by the quality of these wines that you should judge the standing of a shipper.

White Wines

The fermentation of the white grapes usually includes all the pulp, plus the stalks, which provide the essential acids for the wine. In contrast to the red wines, the whites need a long opening fermentation, in cask for the finer wines, and in vat for the lesser appellations.

It is possible for the secondary malo-lactic fermentation to be carried on actually during the first fermentation and whatever happens the cellars are kept warm, so as to keep the wines in a constant state of chemical movement.

Normally, white wines will be bottled earlier than the reds, but this is an individual decision as to the style required, and is dictated by the experience and skill of the producer.

Variations in Burgundy

I hope these insights into the world of growers' and négociants' problems will interest the reader. But to comply with the laws of the A.C., there are many individual winemaking decisions, such as: when to pick' how much to include in the fermentation; how long to ferment; what treatments, within the permitted limits, to make; when to bottle. These will vary from cellar to cellar and therefore from grower to grower. There can be marked differences in the wines within one appellation and even one vineyard. Monsieur X and Monsieur Y may well own an equal share in a fine vineyard—say, Les Poruzots in Meursault—but their wines will be sufficiently different so that one can never be dogmatic as to whether Les Poruzots is 'more dry' or 'firm' or 'subtle' than, for example, the neighbouring vineyard Goutte d'Or. This is one of the things that makes it impossible to lay down the law about Burgundy—and one of the exasperations of the merchant whose customers arrive with fixed ideas as to what certain wines 'ought' to be like!

Vintages

On a journey in Burgundy old wines will be rare, except in the smartest restaurants for over 200 francs per bottle, with added likely faults resulting from rushed service, possible poor storage conditions and no breathing. Generally, restaurants in Burgundy will be offering mainly 1972, 1973 and 1974 vintages, with 1975 introduced following the bottling in early 1977. For the vintage hunter of old wines, seek out 1966, 1964, 1962, 1961 and 1959 of the finer red wines.

Guides to vintages may be helpful but they must be treated with due care and attention. Early pronouncements about vintages can be tinged with commercial interest yet, to be fair, it is possible that more often styles will change during the ageing in cask or vat, and during the development in bottle.

In recent vintages, for example, 1970 was immediately classified for red wines as light and fruity, advanced and to be consumed within three to four years of the vintage. But now many 1970s are proving delightful wines.

OFF-VINTAGES

If a wine of a genuine off-vintage is offered under a known label, it is worth while for the serious wine lover to take the hint and try it because it is quite possible for interesting wines to be made by accident of rainfall in one region or its absence in another, early or late picking of grapes, age of the vines and similar variable influences on viticulture. My message is—do not be too vintage-conscious until many years bring you to the point of familiarity with the variety within one vintage.

Actually, white wines are more liable to be successful in poor vintages than red. 1963 white wines (up until 1973) still demonstrated this with many fine bottles admittedly from the great sites of Montrachet and Corton Charlemagne.

1969. A below-average crop succeeded in producing very high quality red wines. The lighter style of the Côte de Beaune reds are drinking well in 1977, but the finest of the Côte de Nuits can still be kept for a few years. Among white wines the vintage is becoming a little old, except for the finest growths in Puligny.

1970. Very large quantities of wine were made in all areas and, while first appraisals reported pale wines, albeit with a fruity texture, they were often thought to be short of stamina. Since then, however, better-made wines have definitely prolonged their life and 1970 is a vintage that can be enjoyed now. Given correct storage, the 1970 reds could last a few years longer.

The white 1970s also suffered from a lack of body, but during their lifetime they had considerable acclaim. Now there is a tendency for them to maderize, and care should certainly be taken before ordering them. If you are not sure that the wine-maker named on the labels makes quality wines capable of attaining a long life, then go for something younger.

1971. The only trouble with this vintage is the lack of it! Superbly rich, elegant red wines were made, balancing equal levels of acidity and fruit. The smaller wines are coming round now, in 1977, but those bearing any important appellation will need several years maturing to obtain the concentration of the bouquet, and the finesse to linger on the palate which is the hallmark of a great wine.

1972. Here is a vintage about which doors must still be left open. In the first tastings of the reds there was plenty of hardness of flavour, caused by an excess of tannin sufficient to convince many shippers that they would always be too tough to enjoy. Recently samples have shown that this toughness has given way to full-blooded wines softening rapidly.

To say how much this has occurred throughout Burgundy would require an enormous and wide range of tasting, but late in 1976 a 1972 Chassagne Montrachet l'Abbaye de Morgeot Clos de la Chapelle and a 1972 Pommard Épeneaux were delicious for their ripe generosity. By contrast, a 1972 Beaune Aigrots Tasteviné was still over-acidic and unlikely ever to emerge from its closed personality. Red 1972s are quite well stocked in the U.K., so we hope the majority do come round.

The white 1972s are powerfully built with typical and pleasing flavour as long as their acidity is worked out. This is a good vintage with which to gain a first impression of white Burgundy, particularly if you can look at some lesser wines; I have been very pleased with the following: Montagny, St. Aubin, Santenay and Pernand Vergelesses.

1973. This is another vintage of record production which began to come on the market late in 1976. The size of the crop created problems of fermentation because space for the huge quantity and low sugar levels meant more chaptalisation than is usually beneficial. Qualities are mixed—the best will be pleasant drinking over the next few years.

This vintage is more important for white wines where we should see some great bottles from Meursault and Puligny Montrachet. Leave them another year or two, until late 1977 or 1978, before they are brought to the table at their peak.

1974. There were high hopes for the vintage until heavy rain during the picking spoiled the forecast. So far, I have only tasted wines in wood or vat prior to bottling. The general impression is depth of colour and softness with a natural halt to this progress after bottling. An excellent vintage for the white wines, showing real elegance and charm.

1975. The weather conditions were very similar to those of 1974: a hot summer with heavy rains and hail late on caused some rot in the grapes, and this in turn reduced the amount of wine produced. When seeking *négociants'* opinions, I have found a guarded optimism about the ultimate quality. It is felt that great care will be needed in buying, which obviously indicates that they have had some vinification problems; these may have been solved by some growers and not by others, so that the consumer will have to keep in touch with a trusted supplier.

Again with regard to the white wines, we are faced with an outstanding vintage, making the third in succession (which is almost unprecedented). In fact, since 1968 there has not been a bad year for white wines. World demand is now sufficient not to have created a stock surplus, so prices remain firm with an upward graph line.

Other Burgundy Drinks

Cassis Liqueur. A very dark, almost purple liqueur is made from blackcurrants—the French for blackcurrant is '*cassis*'. It is intensely sweet, but more fruity in taste than syrupy. Cassis is used in a number of ways: to flavour puddings and sorbets, marinaded blackcurrants are poured over ice cream, and cassis will enrich many of the confections so magnificently displayed in the shops. The best cassis is made in and around Dijon—Lejay Legoute and Vedrenne are among the best known.

Kir or Vin Blanc Cassis. Possibly the most famous use for cassis liqueur is to make the apéritif known as '*un Kir*' or '*vin blanc cassis*'. Traditionally, this is one-third cassis to which is added two-thirds of chilled Bourgogne Aligoté; it is served in a large glass, with no ice. The effect of pairing a sweet liqueur with a sharp, slightly acidic dry white wine is sensationally thirst-quenching.

The nickname '*un Kir*' comes from the late Canon Félix Kir, a tiny little man who was at one time Mayor of Dijon and a member of the Chamber of Deputies. He played a heroic part in the Resistance during the Second World War and out of affection and respect for him his favourite apéritif was re-named 'Kir' as a delightful memorial to a great man.

Bourgogne Mousseux. To qualify for the description '*Bourgogne mousseux*' or sparkling white Burgundy, the sparkling wine must contain at least 30 per cent of Bourgogne Blanc wine made from the Chardonnay grape. The main centres of production are Rully in the Côte Chalonnaise and Nuits St. Georges. Most Bourgogne mousseux will be qualified by the words '*Méthode Champenoise*', this phrase indicating another *appellation* requirement in that the Mousseux will have been prepared by the same process as Champagne (secondary fermentation taking place in bottle), but with plain Mousseux the wine can be sold when only nine months old, instead of two years as in Champagne.

The expression '*Blanc de Blancs*' will sometimes be used on the label to show that the juice of white grapes only has been used to make the *cuve*. The phrase is not of much importance in this context.

Mousseux can also be used to create a sparkling vin blanc cassis and most restaurants and bars will serve this sparkling apéritif by the glass.

Sparkling Red Burgundy. The fashion for sparkling red Burgundy fell away sharply after the Second World War, partly perhaps because the world of which it was part also ceased to exist. Its reputation in the U.K. was made during Edwardian times and satisfied the late-night drinking of many habitués of the music hall. Nonetheless, there has been a revival in the popularity of certain brands of sparkling red Burgundy in the U.S.A., Canada and countries of southern America. There is still a substantial amount drunk, too, in the north of England.

Production follows the 'Champagne method' and only wines entitled to the Bourgogne Rouge A.C. may be used. Geisweiler could be singled out as a leading shipper, followed by Chauvenet, both of them at Nuits St. Georges.

Best described as a 'fun'. drink, it can be quite useful for parties or buffets where a change from the normal helps the gaiety along.

Marc de Bourgogne. Here we have the local *digestif,* which is taken very seriously by the cognoscenti—mostly from outside the region. Marc de Bourgogne is the local brandy, distilled from all the mush that is left over after the final pressings —stalks, skins, grape pulp and bits in general. It is distilled by mobile stills, under strict government control and, by law, this has to be done in a public place. The result, when aged in oak casks, can be extremely fiery, and it is not the tipple for sensitive stomachs. But if you have a strong constitution, the aroma will fill your head and the subsequent unsubtle flavour will seem to set your soul alight—and a few other places besides. However, devotees insist on its presence after lunch and dinner, preferring the following labels: Louis Latour, Bouchard Père et Fils, Belin, and Hospices de Beaune.

Fine Bourgogne. This is the distillation of Burgundian wine, and not the debris of the pressings as with the Marc, and it is certainly a more refined spirit. Fine Bourgogne is a local curiosity of limited appeal, but worth a try on the spot.

Conclusion

Vintage charts, reports, guides or what have you, are always open to criticism, as undoubtedly my own will be.

Look out for the off-vintage, gradually learn to trust the shippers whose wines you enjoy by recording the taste impressions. It is no value to follow blindly one shipper or group of shippers because 'you are told X is a fine shipper'. Discover for yourself—do not accept reputations that can be commercially advanced without quality. Decide for yourself, remain open-minded, be critical and be reasonable enough to change your mind with grace. After all, Burgundy is fun.

4
Bottles, Labels and Buying

Before attempting to understand the labels of Burgundy wines, it is imperative to recognise the shape of the principal bottle. The sloped neck of this type of bottle is not exclusive to Burgundy, and although the shape is generally referred to as the Burgundy bottle it is in use in other wine regions, principally the Loire and the Rhône.

In the vast wine areas of the south of France (Hérault, Roussillon, Languedoc, etc.) there seems to be no tradition regarding the shape of the bottles used, so that the Burgundy shape will mix with the Bordeaux bottle (with its squared shoulders) and the Hollandaise (dumpy, with a long neck).

The various sizes of bottles found regularly in Burgundy are:

Magnum. This holds two bottles and is usually 1.50 litres in capacity. The magnum size is much less prevalent in Burgundy than in the Bordeaux region, though undoubtedly its use is on the increase as people are buying more big bottles today.

Bottle. This holds 75 cl, 73 cl or 70 cl. All French-bottled wines must carry the contents of the particular size on the label, usually in the left or right bottom corner. Until recently, Burgundy bottles were traditionally of the 75 cl size, holding three-quarters of a litre, and this is still true as regards many wines. Modern legislation, however, has become more precise in what its requirements are for measuring the contents of bottles. This has resulted in some bottles, which are marked 75 cl on the foot of the bottle in the glass, being only 73 cl in their actual contents. In fact, the 73 cl content is probably the most accurate—the cork takes up space and, with time, the wine may become slightly ullaged. The ullage is the air space between the cork and the surface of the wine, which may increase due to slight evaporation.

When inflation and increased duties, plus VAT, pushed the price of cheaper wines upwards in the U.K., a number of shipping firms started to offer their wines in 70 cl bottles, which in appearance are the same yet the bottle provides a half glass of wine less. All these bottles are marked as to their *contenance*

35

(liquid capacity), though less obviously than full-blown consumer protection may deem desirable.

Half bottle. This holds 37.5 cl or 35 cl. In most cases it is an unsatisfactory size—too small for some, too much for others, and certainly not enough for two people. It can be some use as an apéritif size to lead on to bigger things.

Echantillon. This is the name for a trade sample—a tiny bottle.

Labels

First, it must be stated firmly that anyone with a spark of interest in Burgundy wines needs to be able to achieve instant recall of a number of things when viewing bottles in shops or, more quickly still, when shown bottles in a restaurant.

A label can never tell you exactly what the Burgundy tastes like. Remember never to drink labels—just because the name, presentation and vintage appear great, do not automatically assume that the taste of the wine will be equally great. Always go directly to the wine—let it speak for itself. Leave your critical consciousness open and do not be overimpressed by 'get-up'. Certainly in Burgundy the best dressed bottles often contain the dreariest wines and, conversely, the finest wines may sport the dingiest and least imaginative labels.

Most Burgundy bottles have two labels, a neck label (*collarette*) and a body label (*l'étiquette*).

The neck label gives the vintage or sometimes the letters V.S.R. instead of a date. This indicates a non-vintage blended wine; the letters stand for *Vin Spécialement Recommandé* (particularly recommended wine).

Other information on the neck label may be: the name of the shipper and/or négociant (growers rarely put their name on the neck label); meaningless expressions meant as descriptions that are as yet uncontrolled and are intended to give the wine commercial appeal—e.g. 'Grand Vin (de Bourgogne)', 'Grand Vin de Réserve', 'Vin Supérieur'.

The neck label, necklet or collarette should really just indicate the vintage and the shipper.

The body label is central to this subject for, from it, the significant information will be available. Firstly, it bears the name of the wine, and you should note very clearly that any wine grown in Burgundy and offered as Burgundy must be an *appellation contrôlée* wine coming from one of the Burgundy A.C.s listed (page 119). On this list there are generic wines (such as Bourgogne Rouge/Blanc), sometimes qualified by a *marque déposée* (trade mark), for example A.C. Bourgogne Blanc 'Comte de Chartogne' from the firm of Jaboulet-Vercherre.

It may be a village wine from a legally delimited area, for example Nuits St. Georges. It may be a village wine plus the specific vineyard from that village, for example Volnay Clos des Chênes. It may be a vineyard so famous and historically fine that it has earned its own *appellation*, for example Le Musigny, from Chambolle Musigny. Here the words Chambolle Musigny are not obligatory on the label. An extra example in this context is Bonnes Mares, a vineyard of its own that straddles two village *appellations contrôlées*, Morey St. Denis and Chambolle Musigny.

Many Burgundy firms offer wines where the label shows no A.C. and this can be taken to imply that they are wines blended to resemble Burgundy styles but fetching far lower prices. They are marketed to satisfy some of the local demand and even the export trade that will hope to supply carafe wines in a Burgundy style. Brand names proliferate in this category.

Shipper/Négociant/Grower/Domaine Names

In the U.K., the shipper's name may be a U.K.-based firm, such as Sichel, Corney and Barrow, or—my own firm, Laytons. It is permissible to register firms' names in Beaune, Nuits St. Georges, etc. in order to use the label for export, and some of us make our own cellarage arrangements in the region as an operating base. In my case, we use Marcel Amance et Cie. in Santenay. "Trust the shipper, my boy" has been a reasonable attitude to adopt, but it is somewhat superficial if Burgundy is to be judged by higher standards of critical perception.

A shipper should visit the Burgundy region several times each year if he is to work significantly with his suppliers. Such bottles as he offers will be qualified by '*Mise en bouteilles en Bourgogne*', 'Bottled in France', 'Bottled in the region of production'.

The *négotiant* is the French shipper. The town or village where he has his office and main cellars must be mentioned after his name. For example:

> Louis Latour (Beaune)
> Bouchard Père et Fils (Beaune)
> Faiveley (Nuits St. Georges)
> Henri de Villamont (Savigny-lès-Beaune)
> Prosper Maufoux (Santenay)

It is the firms of *négociants* that remain the backbone of the Burgundy wine trade: their names will need to be mastered before a full knowledge of Burgundy labels can be claimed. Usually the corks are branded, most commonly by '*Mise en bouteilles dans la région de production*' (bottled in the region of production).

With the growth of bottling by the grower, more wines will be seen in the various chains of distribution with their own label. To identify such a label, look for an individual name, as opposed to that of a firm. Quite often the label will also say '*Mise du propriétaire*', '*Mise à la propriété*', or '*Mis en bouteilles par le propriétaire*'. All mean 'Bottled by the proprietor (grower)'.

A *domaine* can be defined as several vineyards, possibly in

various villages, singly owned, but of course vinified separately
to maintain a scrupulous division between the different A.C.s
that may be involved. These wines are bottled by the domaine
and sold under such a label. For example: Domaine Parent,
propriétaire à Pommard (Côte d'Or). Apart from Pommard,
this domaine also owns vineyards in Beaune, Volnay,
Monthélie and Corton.

Domaine labels will be qualified by '*Mise du domaine*', '*Mise au
domaine*', '*Mis en bouteilles au domaine*'—all meaning 'Domaine
bottled'.

It may have been thought unnecessary to note a difference
between a grower and a domaine, but there are some minor
points to note. Firstly, a domaine will own a larger area of vines
than a grower; secondly, a domaine will be more likely to bottle its own wines than a grower; and, thirdly, a domaine may be
managed on behalf of shareholders.

OTHER LABEL INFORMATION

The vintage year may be shown on the label, although it is
more usual to have it printed on the neck label. The quantity of
wine held in the bottle will be expressed in centilitres.

The various sizes of lettering on labels are controlled by the
French labelling laws, although these need not concern us.
They do ensure that no wine name that should be clearly shown
is in any way detracted from by any other name or word.

One of the first achievements for a new buyer is to recognise
the 'phoney' or 'bent' label. There are a few U.K. shippers
attempting to pass off bottles from the Burgundy region as
'French bottled' when, by a study of the label, it is clear that
they are not. The misleading expressions used are:

'*Mis en bouteilles dans nos caves*' (it depends where the 'caves'
are, London or Beaune?) and '*Mis par l'acheteur*' (yes, but where
did the buyer do the bottling?). This practice is not widespread,
but in every trade there are a few small firms prepared to
chance their integrity for positive commercial gain.

SUMMARY

The complete information required concerning the wine
should be available on the Burgundy label. It comprises:

The name—generic, village and/or vineyard;

The responsible person—foreign shipper, *négociant*, grower
or *domaine*;

Vintage—the year of production;

Size of bottle—contents measure.

Certain traditional label expressions used to indicate the
quality of the wine as considered by the grower or shipper.
These are now largely historic and in my opinion it is best to ig-
nore: '*Tête de Cuvée*', '*Première Cuvée*', and '*Vieille(s) Vigne(s)*'.

Another qualifying expression, '*Premier Cru*', must be treated with caution, as there have been attempts at several classifications of Côte d'Or vineyards. Whilst the top vineyards appear in each, there are some sites claiming *Premier Cru* status without complete authority to do so. Occasionally a village name will be followed by '*Premier Cru*' or '*1er Cru*' (the same thing) and no vineyard name. This means that two *Premier Cru* vineyard wines of the same village have been blended together and so the wine loses its claim to a vineyard name but retains its *Premier Cru* entitlement.

Reading a Burgundy label is something that will repay anyone, whether in terms of the quality of wine you get or the money—and disappointments—that you are saved. Nor is it really difficult: indeed, you should look very sharply at any label that does confuse you. Sort out the information the label gives and interpret it according to the facts. Then you will know something definite about what the bottle contains. But never forget that no label can guarantee quality; this is the sole responsibility of the person who grew and made the wine, the firm who bought and shipped it, and, eventually, the merchant who offers it. His name and his alone is your 'guarantee'.

How to buy Burgundy

When you're in the region of Burgundy itself, don't be carried away by your enjoyment of the wines so that you're easily persuaded to pay fancy prices. If you can pause to do some basic calculations, preferably with one or two good British wine lists for immediate comparison, you'll often find that you should wait to do your buying until you get home. This has the advantage that, not only may you actually save on the purchase price, but also you will be able to follow up with a personal query, should you think there is anything wrong with the wines.

There are two new retail wine shops in Beaune, stocking a wide range of wines from a good selection of bottles appropriately chosen as likely to appeal to the wine-lover seeking a souvenir. These are Denis Perret, offering wines from five firms, Drouhin, Bouchard Père et Fils, Louis Latour, Louis Jadot and Chanson Père et Fils, and the Vinothèque, which is totally independent. If you visit a cellar or tourist tasting room, there will usually be some inducement for you to buy wine, generally in a pack of three or six bottles in a specially designed carton. Again, don't rush to buy: a little mental arithmetic will quickly tell you the value—or otherwise.

But to buy Burgundy in Britain, whether for drinking immediately or for laying down for long-term maturation, it is essential to discover a wine merchant who both knows the subject and who can sincerely enthuse about his stocks of this somewhat complex wine. It isn't all that difficult.

You can't buy Burgundy just by picking a name off a list. There must be some personal contact between you and the supplier. Write to or telephone the merchant—ideally, get to know him by visiting him at his place of business. If he holds tastings of Burgundies, this is an even easier way of establishing a relationship. Don't be shy about wanting to find out about him and why he lists the Burgundies he does: ask him how many times he has been to Burgundy—and when he was last there. A man who merely did a session there as a trainee twenty years ago is hardly likely to be alert to the possibilities and problems of the present time; someone who makes regular visits or who is in constant contact with one or more of the shippers will know about current trends and how wines of particular growers and *négociants* may suit his public. If you can get your merchant to talk to you, you can soon judge as to whether his command of the subject is deep and sincere or not.

BUYING OLD WINES

A word of warning to the wealthy who may be tempted by offers of very old vintages of Burgundy. These wines can be wonderful buys (however much you may have to pay for them) if—and it is an important "if"—they have been kept in the same cellar throughout their period of maturation. Be somewhat wary of wines that have an old vintage date on their labels but that have been recently shipped from Burgundy. It is highly probable that the natural deposit that forms, and should form, in the bottle of such fine wines may have been extracted by a mechanical device and the bottle re-corked prior to shipment. This is done with good intent. Many export markets—notably the United States (but not the U.K.)—suspect any kind of sediment in a bottle of wine, and refuse wines with 'bits' in them, so that the Burgundians endeavour to give them star-bright wines.

Frankly, I think that this practice of removing the deposit, on which the wine feeds throughout its life in bottle, simply extracts the guts of the wine, and a beverage that is weak and thin in flavour replaces one that might have possessed grandeur if it had been left alone. So try, if you buy such wines, to ascertain that this 'decanting' has not taken place. This is another reason for getting to know a wine merchant, who will have the detailed knowledge of where your wines have been and how they have been kept!

HOW I BUY BURGUNDY—AS A BURGUNDY SHIPPER

The British market faces special problems with Burgundy, and these are unlikely to be solved within a year or two. Competing as we do with other export markets that have strong traditions for buying and appreciating Burgundy, such as Belgium, The Netherlands, Switzerland and, now, the United States, the present weakness of the pound sterling puts Britain at a great disadvantage. It is no use listing wines that are simply too expensive for the public to begin to think about buying them!

Whether or not the U.K. can remain an important and respected market for the wines of Burgundy—as it has been in the past—must now depend on how individual British shippers are able to give up time far in excess of what may be economic for their firms or, indeed, convenient for them as human beings, so as to search out stocks of wines that their countrymen can both like and afford. They must, too, circumvent various old methods of buying that are simply too costly. For example, no British Burgundy shipper these days can rely on simply receiving samples and tasting these in the offices of his principal, or on depending on what his interpreter may tell him as regards prices and qualities of wines when he travels in the country. He must make his own assessment as to the calibre of the source of supply, and impress such sources with his own abilities in being able to promote and handle the wines they may be offering him: if he can't hold his own in a business discussion with a peasant proprietor or a broker, he risks paying a higher price than he can really afford, not because of any sharp practice but simply because he is at a disadvantage now as regards money and must therefore stress his assets of know-how and prestige.

Personally, as a London-based shipper, conducting my own Burgundy business, I enjoy the constant challenge to me, as an individual. I would not want to be just an agent for one single Burgundy house, as the restrictions on my activities would be too tight for me to operate in the way I think is most effective for my organisation—and my customers.

A digression on my buying philosophy may be relevant, if it helps the reader to understand how these precious wines reach the lists of my firm. First, it's essential and prudent to establish firm and happy business relationships, in which each party has respect for the other. Spread friendship far and wide, always.

For firms who have limited resources of capital, it is a requirement not to hold large stocks of wine these days, but to seek suppliers who themselves are able to bear the responsibility and financial burden of stock continuity or maturation: to ensure continuity, stocks have to be held—and capital tied up —for a considerable time. In this context, the *négociant* fills the role of the ideal supplier; usually, such a shipper can also offer a more commercial approach to business transactions, by more fully understanding the business problems that are certainly attached to the operations of the British wine trade today.

In the case of my own firm, our Burgundy trade has developed sufficiently for us to have our own establishment in Santenay (where many of our wines are bottled), with Pierre Maufoux in the firm of Marcel Amance. Yet we—my colleagues and I—still continue to visit many other *négociants*, in order to search out bargains, appraise different styles of wines, and gain knowledge of ranges from which we can select wines of greater variety for our customers.

For me, to visit the cellars of growers, together with my broker and/or *négociant*, so as to taste the wines and make a selection, is the main work with which I, as a shipper, am really concerned. Others have different ways of doing business, and whether the result is good or bad is their affair.

Decanting Burgundy—or not

Travellers in Burgundy are sometimes surprised that, on occasions when really fine wines are served, these are poured straight from the bottle. If you want your wine decanted, you may have to insist, for the wine waiter won't ask you if you want it done and he may point out that there isn't any deposit so why are you worrying? Even when you've got your way, he may have to go and look for a decanter—or ask you if you mind the wine being simply decanted into a clean bottle, or the original bottle, rinsed free of its deposit.

Why don't the Burgundians decant their wines? The previous paragraph gives some clue. Although in a luxurious eating-place, catering mainly for the sort of tourists who demand international food and often welcome what is sometimes referred to as '*le grand chi-chi*' of service, decanting may be done, in general it won't be, simply because the average Burgundian may not have what we understand by 'decanters'.

The Burgundian wine producer is, for the most part, a real countryman, in other words, a farmer, and he lives simply, spending money on essentials—which certainly include food and drink—but avoiding extravagance. His home is usually above his cellar and, when he wants wine, he goes and fetches a bottle and, after drawing the cork, puts it on the table. There is no elaborate service by house servants and, in the majority of restaurants, the staff (who may often be the owner's family) will be friendly and simple, rather than professionally smooth; this does not, I must admit, include the students of the various catering schools, such as that of Tournus, who serve the banquets of Burgundy, for example some of those given at Les Trois Glorieuses, and who impress by their adept and wholly skilled presentation of dishes.

Incidentally, one of the possible reasons for the use in Burgundy of the enormous glasses that may, filled, hold one or more whole bottles of wine is, I suggest, so that the wine in such a glass may receive the aeration that it might otherwise get by pouring it into a decanter. But this doesn't make me like giant glasses any better: the excessive airing that a wine receives when it is swung round in something the size (and shape) of a storm lantern can sometimes result in it throwing off all its bouquet before the drinker gets more than a vague whiff of it! These giant glasses, sometimes brought out with much fuss, for a special—and expensive—red Burgundy, are really gimmicks developed by restaurants catering for the sort of clientele that knows very little about wine, but likes a show to be made.

There are other possible reasons why the practice of decanting has never been much followed in Burgundy. I have found the deposit in Burgundies to be firm, rather than in fine particles, so that, if one pours carefully from a bottle, without tilting it up and down and stirring up the sediment, this deposit will remain in the last of the wine. But the French don't seem to mind it being in their glasses either and, maybe on account of their habitual thrift or because they think Anglo-Saxons are fussy about preferring wine to be bright and clear in appearance, they will tip out every scrap from a bottle, deposit and all! With red Bordeaux, the fineness of some of the deposit can make a wine cloudy if it is not carefully decanted, but this has not been my experience with even oldish red Burgundies.

It may be—and one can only go by personal experience —that some Burgundies do not benefit from being decanted. I once was serving a fine Burgundy in magnums, which I had decanted, and the wine was so good that I had to go down to my cellar and get some bottles up, which I was obliged to serve immediately after drawing the corks. My guests all found the wine poured straight from the bottles much better! But this is the sort of thing that shows how impossible it is to make definite and general statements about Burgundy: each set of circumstances can make one change one's mind, and every fine wine can require different treatment. You must go on tasting and experimenting and realise that it is impossible ever to be definite about the best way to serve this wine—only to try and avoid risking the bottle being spoiled by careless handling.

5
Burgundy
Wine Journey

You really need a car to explore Burgundy, because the vineyards are essentially part of the real countryside. So it is worth while hiring one, even for a day or two, during a sojourn there. Excursions through the vineyards can be undertaken by means of the tours organised by the Office du Toursime and the Syndicat d'Initiative in Beaune.

Of course, no one can expect to see everything, even if several days or weeks are available, and naturally much depends on whether you are going to include visiting the many historic and architectural treasures in which Burgundy is rich, as well as looking at vineyards. I would not, anyway, suggest a hurried tour: you need to survey the landscape, observe the way in which the colour of the vineyard soil changes in different regions, note the curves and hollows of the plots, and bear in mind all that this may imply in terms of the wine that is being produced there. Take time to stop the car, study the vineyards both close to and from a distance, even if you are doing this in winter when the vines themselves look bare and dead. But look at the way in which the vineyards make a pattern, with the stone houses and farm buildings, and register this when you stand beside some quite small area planted with vines that make world-famous bottles of wine, possibly beyond your pocket except for special occasions. If you do this in the heart of Burgundy, you will never feel quite the same about the wines again.

In each of the following sections, I have described something of the wines and specific vineyards, but you must make your own choice of routes and follow your own inclinations as to places to stop. You are specially recommended to buy Michelin maps numbers 66 and 71, and maps 61 and 65 for the Chablis area. The green Michelin Guide *Bourgogne* will assist with many places of general interest.

Possible Itineraries

If you have a whole day, the first itinerary will show you the en-

44

tire Côte de Beaune. To follow it, leave Beaune on the N6 and, after about a mile, turn off to the right on the N73. After the branch-off, you will be able to see Pommard, Volnay, Monthélie, Auxey Duresses, Meursault, Puligny, Chassagne and Santenay.

If you have only a half day available and also want to see something of the town of Beaune itself, follow the same route but, after Puligny, take the main road back (N6) to Beaune. If you are making the whole circuit (during which you can probably break for lunch in either Auxey or Meursault), you will also return to Beaune by the N6.

For another whole day, you should see the Côte de Nuits. You could do this in half a day by making an early morning start and by not stopping along the way, although to rush through in this way would obviously be a pity. Leave Beaune by the Porte St. Nicolas, and as if you were going along the old N6 to Dijon. At the first set of traffic lights, the road will lead you over the Haute Côte de Nuits, through the top of the Bois de Corton, and bring you down at Nuits St. Georges. From Nuits St. Georges you can join the N6 again, going north and seeing Vosne, going off this route at Vougeot, following the vineyard road so that you can see Chambolle, Morey, Gevrey, Fixin and Marsannay. After this, you can return to Beaune on the new fast motor route.

Another whole day is necessary to see Chablis. For this, you take the motorway, and, after about two hours' drive, leave it at Auxerre Sud, and follow the signposts for Chablis, returning afterwards by the same route.

For anyone really short of time, the Beaune vineyard will at least give the visitor some idea of Burgundy. You can take the road out of town and go in the direction of the Montagne de Beaune and Bouze-lès-Beaune, and from this site enjoy a panorama of the vineyards. It can be easily done in an hour by car and it is a very pleasant excursion on foot, either if you take the car part of the way or actually walk from Beaune.

If you have already explored part of Burgundy, Aloxe-Corton and the northern end of the Côte de Beaune provide a very interesting itinerary, because the wines are now becoming widely known. The trip can be easily managed within a couple of hours, and allows the traveller to pay homage to the Corton Charlemagne vineyard en route. Leave Beaune by the Porte St. Nicolas, following the RN74 to Aloxe-Corton, and then follow the itinerary suggested (page 56).

Another excursion can take half a day, or be extended for a whole day if you lunch en route and then devote an afternoon to seeing some of the art treasures and monuments such as Cluny, Tournus and the countryside in general. For this, you leave Beaune on the N6, going south, and, at Chagny, you take the N481 in the centre of the town down to Buxy, returning via Montagny, Mercurey and Rully. This part of the journey will

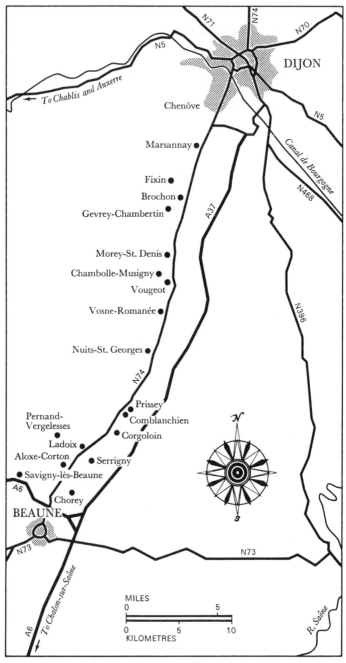

The Burgundy Region—Dijon/Beaune

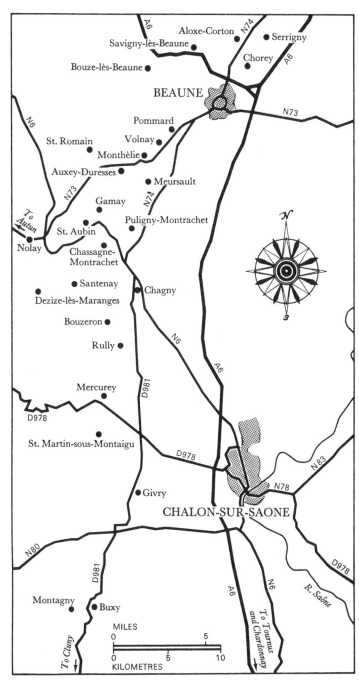

The Burgundy Region—Beaune/Chalon-sur-Saône

only take about half a day, unless you make several stops.

Anyone staying in Dijon must see the Ancient Palais des Ducs de Bourgogne, which is now the Musée des Beaux Arts. The Musée Perrin de Puycousin has an exhibition of objects relating to local life in Dijon and Tournus, and the Cellier de Clairvaux, built in the thirteenth century, is a regional tasting room.

Try to allow a whole day to see Beaune, an attractive little town, where you can walk right round inside the old walls. Things of particular interest are, of course, the Hospices de Beaune, which is also known as l'Hôtel-Dieu and Musée (if you simply enquire for the 'Hospices', you may not be directed helpfully). The Musée du Vin de Bourgogne is in the former Hôtel des Ducs de Bourgogne and shows every aspect of wine production, together with an interesting collection of tastevins, and the famous tapestry by Lurçat, showing wine, the source of life, triumphing over death. Among the many other works of art and things of historic interest, the tapestries in the Eglise Notre Dame should not be missed. In the narrow streets, both picturesque and apparently unchanged, which lead off from the Place Carnot and Hôtel de Ville, you can wander about for hours. It goes without saying that the various shops, especially those dealing in food, around the Place Carnot and the Place du Marché, are irresistible for the gastronomic traveller.

Chablis

Chablis is a small town and a small wine region in the Département de l'Yonne, producing exclusively dry white wines in varying qualities from the grandest, with its uniquely chalky flavour, down to the refreshing modest carafe wine sold by the *pichet* (or small jug) in the local restaurant. It has been called the "golden gate to Burgundy".

For the traveller going south, by car, Chablis is the first region of Burgundy. The *Autoroute du Sud* (A6) passes the area, with a conveniently signposted exit after two hours driving from Paris. Chablis lies some ten kilometres east of the *autoroute*, yet it retains the atmosphere aptly described as "*île vineuse*" (wine island). The region is indeed a definite wine island, ten miles long four miles wide, running roughly north to south. Today, however, it is of much less importance than during the Middle Ages, when this whole area, Lower Burgundy, extended to the then large viticultural districts around the towns of Avallon, Joigny, Tonnerre and Irancy. The wines they make today are rarely seen outside the immediate vicinity.

By studying the map, you will see that the Chablis region is much nearer to the southern end of the Champagne district than it is to the Burgundy heart in the Côte d'Or, centred on Beaune. Indeed, the fringe vineyards of Champagne are only 15 miles from Chablis, whilst the Côte d'Or is some 65 miles further down the *autoroute*. 'Chablis', as a generic title, gives its

name to the wines from the many villages and hamlets surrounding the town, the starting point for all visits.

THE TOWN

First-time visitors will be surprised to find Chablis a small town
for such a famous one—yet it is much the better for that, and is
virtually unspoiled by twentieth-century developments. The
Church of St. Martin, first built in 1160, indicates to some extent the history of Chablis. The town was owned by the French
Crown until the ninth-century when it was gifted to the Church
of St. Martin at Tours, in the Loire. It remained in religious
possession until 1789, when the French Revolution broke up
the freehold ownerships.

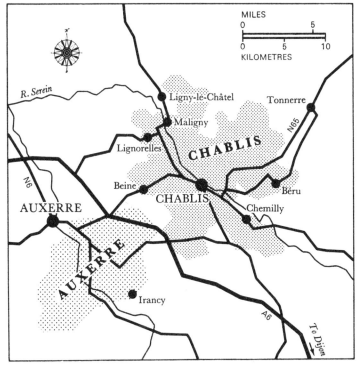

Chablis

For the *gastronome* or *gourmand* (the 'discriminating', or just
'greedy') the Hôtel de l'Étoile, owned by the Bergerand family
since 1848, offers the choice of *haute cuisine* and a fine selection
of Chablis wines not to be missed if the pocket, perhaps even
more than the stomach, can stand the strain. Otherwise you can
eat more modestly in the humbler cafés and restaurants.

WHAT ARE THE WINES LIKE?

It is hard to marshal sufficient adjectives to give an accurate
description of the wines, because the lively spirit of Chablis is so

exclusive; yet this seems to pass unnoticed by the inhabitants of the region, situated away from the main Burgundy area. Its insular nature is, perhaps, matched by the insularity felt by a stranger. Chablis does feel isolated—the growers only discuss Chablis and appear to know little of the outside world and wines—and they allow no other white wines even the possibility of being better than theirs.

Never, then, compare Chablis with other white Burgundies, for the latter do not have the steely dryness and delicious acidity, wrapped around the strength of flavour, that develops in the best quality Chablis after two or three years in bottle. These qualities will obviously be found in varying degrees, from the peak of the seven *Grand Cru* vineyards, through the eleven *Premier Cru* vineyards, down to the plain Chablis and Petit Chablis. The difficulty expressed earlier in helping you to understand the taste of Chablis, requires you to dismiss from your mind all the frightful wines you might have drunk in the past, masquerading as 'Chablis', none of which probably bears the slightest resemblance to the real thing. The historical problems of the labelling of any Burgundy bottled outside of France is discussed elsewhere (page 3). To discover true Chablis wines it is necessary, in my opinion, to buy only those wines bottled in the region of production. I say this with the greatest respect to the great shippers of the Côte d'Or—and, of course, there are some few exceptions. But in general Chablis must be bottled in Chablis, though it is possible to find restaurants serving 'open' wine.

Vineyard ownership is split amongst many *vignerons* and tenants (*rentiers*). Only the dedicated growers will be successful because of the poor quality soil and unreliable weather conditions, which can bring late frosts and hail, and destroy within hours the entire year's crop. The harvest is never safe until it is picked, pressed and in the fermentation vats (*cuves*), during which time chaptalisation is necessary (see page 26). At the vinification, care is needed not to spoil both the character and the delicate balance that is the unique charm of Chablis.

Making Chablis is a struggle, rewarded on average only five years in every ten with a decent vintage. Wines of the Chablis appellation must reach a minimum of 10° of alcohol content. Do not allow them to get too old, although some from the Grand Cru vineyards can age for up to ten years if carefully stored, and if they come from a vintage renowned for youthful power, such as 1969 and 1975. In order to appreciate Chablis in general, allow two to four years maturation in bottle, when the wines will show their distinction more vividly, having lost their initial sharpness.

THE WINES OF CHABLIS

Grand Cru—the finest growths. Looking out from the main

square of Chablis across the little river Serein, a tributary of the Yonne, you can see the seven Grand Cru vineyards joined together in a row facing south: Vaudésir, Preuses, Les Clos, Grenouilles, Bougros, Valmur, Blanchots.

Only in fine vintages will the wines of these vineyards be sold under their own names; otherwise they will be declassified at the decision of the grower down to Premier Cru Chablis, or even straight Chablis. The laws of A.C. require Grand Crus to reach 11°, and, as with all Chablis appellations, the only grape permitted is the 'Chardonnay' (local name, Beaunois). Other grape varieties such as 'Sacy' and 'Aligoté' can be found in the Chablis region, but they can only be used for Bourgogne Grand Ordinaire and Bourgogne Aligoté, respectively.

The flavour of Grand Cru Chablis is special in every respect. For colour, observe the green hues glinting among the golden shadows; smell the wine slowly by inhaling the bouquet after agitating the glass. The taste fills out in the mouth and spreads across the tongue, leaving a delicate aroma within the mouth.

The wines are bottled roughly a year after the vintage, but need another three or four years to reach their peak. The differences in taste between products of the different vineyards can be left to the local experts; however, in my experience, Grenouilles and Les Clos have given me the finest bottles. The average annual production will be only 6,500 cases (a dozen bottles in a case), to satisfy demand both in France and the thirsty world, and remember that in not every year will the wines reach the quality to get the Grand Cru accolade.

Chablis Premier Cru—second growths. The little river Serein is the key to Chablis. You can see the Grand Cru vineyards virtually jostling the town. Now to explore the second most important appellation of Chablis, the *Premier Cru* (although, in fact, the description does not mean 'first' at all, but 'second'.)

Until 1967 there were 22 vineyards scattered along the left and right banks of the Serein entitled to Premier Cru status. This number was reduced to eleven to avoid confusion and the names listed below were retained as the best known.

On the south side of the Serein: Beauroy, Côte de Léchet*, Vaillons*, Melinots, Montmains*, Vosgros. On the north side of the Serein: Fourchaume*, Montée de Tonnerre, Monts de Milieu*, Vaucoupin, Les Fourneaux.

It must be understood that vineyard holdings are very fragmented, leaving little chance for a grower to produce a wine from one single patch of vineyard in any quantity, so this amalgamation of names became necessary to keep to the commercial sales requirements. In fact, the grower retains the right to use the old vineyard name (French logic), or the new name, or even just '*Premier Cru*' without the vineyard name.

*The vineyards producing wines usually seen on the export market.

In offering a tasting description it seems churlish to criticise *Premier Cru* wines at all, though I feel obliged to indicate some essential difference in quality against the *Grand Cru*. Half a degree of alcohol actually separates them, and from the slight reduction results the lesser weight of flavour and more muted highlights. Perhaps, once fully developed, the *Grand Cru* wines will yield more subtlety but this will depend on the tasting undertaken by the individual and his or her tasting memory.

Chablis. Nearly one and a quarter million bottles is the average production of Chablis in good vintages—in comparison with production in other wine regions, this is not much to satisfy the world. As the vineyard area is spread throughout the villages of the near countryside and along the exit roads towards Auxerre, Tonnerre and Maligny, it is striking how the vine has not maintained itself as a predominant feature of the landscape as it was in former times.

The wines that are sold as A.C. straight Chablis never carry a vineyard name, but this is not important. Fragmented vineyard ownership causes growers to blend their wines from possibly several sites. This blending is beneficial, as it enables the grower or shipper to balance his *cuvées* (vatting), which certainly improve when individual merits can be transferred to the wines lying in wood or vat prior to bottling.

When tasting or drinking straight Chablis, it is probable that the first impression will be the taste buds' quick reaction to the acidity of the wine when young. Normally, this will break down with bottle age, but the wine beginner will be aware of the sharpness on the tongue and around the teeth when tasting such youthful wines. This acidity is essential for Chablis, and, as long as it is not excessive, the character of Chablis needs it, if the wine is to remain firm and upright in taste.

Without its natural acidity, Chablis will not live and improve. Do not be afraid of the acidity: it harmonises well with the concentrated cold steel backbone of true Chablis.

The appearance of Chablis has provoked many attempts to describe its colour. You will find it paler and greener, without the slight hay yellow of the *Grand Cru* and *Premier Cru* wines. But, as with them, the taste is gripping and definite.

To find the main villages of the region responsible for the wines of the straight Chablis appellation visit Maligny, Beine, Lignorelles, Chemilly and Bértu. Tastings and cellar visits are possible, but you may have to push yourself forward and certainly either speak in French or try to do so (see Glossary).

The wines for the appellation Chablis are produced exclusively from the Chardonnay grape in the less favoured villages on the perimeter of the Chablis area. They are generally more acidic and less fruity than those wines entitled to the A.C.s *Grand Cru* and *Premier Cru*, which makes them ideal for drinking in their two years of life.

Petit Chablis. Petit Chablis is not a large appellation. It is about a third the size of Chablis and has never been well known in the U.K. The British impression of Petit Chablis is probably false in that many consumers believe that the word 'Petit' is slightly denigrating, and implies an inferior wine. This is not so—agreed, it is less fine than the appellation 'Chablis' and the higher growths, yet Petit Chablis is not at all an inferior wine.

Several growers are now replanting land never under vines since the disaster of phylloxera in the last century, hoping that the growing world demand for Chablis wine may thereby be satisfied in the less affluent countries (the U.K. must at present be included here) which can enjoy the clean, crisp wines of Petit Chablis. A change of title to 'Chablis Villages' has been proposed and this, if adopted, would be welcomed by British shippers.

Bourgogne Aligoté. A small amount of Aligoté is grown near Chablis to make *vin de consommation courante* (wine for everyday drinking). It is dry, with the chalky flavour coming from the Chablis soil. It is different from the Côte d'Or Aligoté, with a marked added crispness and light dancing taste. It is rarely exported, except by the firm of Lamblin of Maligny, who offer it under the label 'Grand Blanc de Lamblin'.

Bourgogne Grand Ordinaire. The white grape variety Sacy is also found in the outer Chablis region, but the wine made from it is entitled only to the appellation Bourgogne Grande Ordinaire. Consumed mostly locally and not often seen on its own, it is sometimes purchased by shippers to contribute a sprightliness to a blend for the A.C. Bourgogne Grande Ordinaire.

Seen locally but rarely exported—the remaining wines of Lower Burgundy:

Irancy: a red wine grown on slopes behind the village of Irancy. It needs much age and is only successful in hot summers. It has a somewhat heavy style.

Coulanges-la-Vineuse: a red wine somewhat similar to Irancy.

St. Bris-le-Vineux: a white wine made from the Sauvignon grape (used in the Loire for Sancerre and Pouilly Fumé). It has a distinctive dry, aromatic bouquet, with a light flavour. This area was taken up some ten years ago by John Harvey of Bristol.

Avallon: white and red wines from the valleys of the Rivers Cure and the Cousin are made, though only the red wines have any real reputation. They are supposedly quite vigorous.

Auxerre: a local, pleasant and dry rosé from this once large vineyard may be found in the restaurants.

All the above vineyard areas are on the south side of the A6—that is, in the direction of Auxerre, the other side from Chablis. To the east of Chablis the town of Tonnerre maintains a few vineyards in the Armançon valley. These produce both red and white wines the quality of which is entirely unknown to me. If any one knows of them, I shall be delighted to learn more.

The whole Chablis vineyard was, as I have said, very much larger in former times. It also seems to have suffered more than other vineyard regions from climatic disasters and diseases. As recently as 1956, a severe frost destroyed so many vines that it was said in Chablis that at least twenty years must pass before production could really recover. Frozen vines must be cleared and the vineyards have to lie fallow to recover. Planting new vineyards after clearing the ground is costly, and the young vines require time to develop and produce. Then there is another three years before the wine can bear an *appellation*. The past twenty years have brought the additional problem of finding labour.

Yet the demand for Chablis—even if it has sometimes been satisfied with the sort of wine that could never be confused with the product of this small Burgundy vineyard for those who know the real thing—continues and increases. I believe that, possibly within the next ten years, this wine region may return to something of its former glory.

The Côte d'Or

Because the traveller will hear constant references to the Côte d'Or, it is important to realise exactly what this is. The viticultural or wine-producing area of Burgundy was defined by decree on 29th April, 1930. This Decree applied to wines grown in the Yonne (Chablis), the Côte d'Or (Côte de Beaune and Côte de Nuits, which are the vineyard areas around the town of Beaune and those that extend from Dijon down into the southwest, just south of Santenay, a distance of 40 miles), The Saône-et-Loire (Côte Chalonnaise and the Mâconnais regions in southern Burgundy), and the Rhône (which in this context does not mean the region of Rhône wines as such, but includes the Beaujolais). This book does not deal with the Mâconnais and Beaujolais regions because of limitations of space.

The Côte d'Or comprises the two *côtes* (slopes) which are internationally famous: the Côte de Nuits (the centre of which is Nuits St. Georges) and the Côte de Beaune (the centre of which is Beaune). The Côte Chalonnaise, immediately to the south of the Côte de Beaune, is not, traditionally, within the Côte d'Or, although the wines of this Côte are usually listed among those of the Côte d'Or for convenience. To divide up the different Burgundy wine regions too much might make for confusion, although the wines do differ greatly in style.

The vineyards of the Côte d'Or extend the full length of 40 miles, and the area is well named the 'golden slopes'. The colour patterns during harvest time and just after are quite sensational and it is a pity that more visitors do not see this region when, after the vintage, the leaves of the vines turn a brilliant red and gold, and are spectacular.

It is important to remember these two distinct areas that, together, make up the Côte d'Or, because the wines from them are in fact very different. The Côte de Nuits begins a few miles to the south of Dijon at Fixin, though the village of Chenove, with its ancient wine press, is the last remaining village of this Côte, and it is now actually in the suburbs of Dijon, where wine is still made. In former times there was also an area in the Côte de Dijon as well, but this began to fall into desuetude after the *phylloxera* plague of the late nineteenth-century and with the expansion of Dijon in the industrial era. Vines were also grown to the north of Dijon, but these have disappeared as well and therefore the Côte de Dijon can be dismissed as something of the past. From Fixin down to Corgoloin and Comblanchien, with its marble quarry, is the area known as the Côte de Nuits, with Nuits St Georges as its main town and centre.

La Côte de Beaune

The Côte de Beaune starts immediately at Ladoix-Serrigny and extends down to Dezize, just past Santenay. Running virtually parallel with the Côte d'Or slopes is the RN74 main road, that now fortunately carries far less traffic as the motorway bears the

View of La Rochepot above the Côte de Beaune

brunt of the heavy lorries. This RN74 is the old road; in the old days, travellers took the Lyon-Paris road, via Beaune and Dijon. It has always seemed to me bad luck for the land owners on the east side of the RN74 that their vineyards don't carry the A.C. entitlement of the vineyards on the west side of this road, that lead up the slopes, as these last are the names that every drinker knows. However, on my last visit to Burgundy I was told by a famous shipper that the opinion is generally held that this road, of such ancient lineage, was made exactly along the line where the quality of wine was noticeably inferior, as more of the vineyards were on the flat. It is certainly noticeable that the soil on each side of the road is very different: on the east side the soil is definitely darker, thicker in texture, more obviously earthy and, indeed, more as you would expect a flat, rather low-lying plot to be. This whole area leads down to the river Saône, which in prehistoric times was a vast inland lake. This is also worth remembering, because the fossils of such places enrich the soil, especially for vines. So it is not difficult to understand that the best wines come only from the slopes between the old road and the hillside or 'côte' itself, the finest growths being concentrated in the positions on the middle slope where they are slightly sheltered and receive the contributory elements of sun, rain and rain drainage, plus enjoying the better soil for vines. Consequently, the vineyard area of the slope is not wide—two miles at the widest and as little as 700 yards at the narrowest.

The visitor to Burgundy will often remark on the serenity and calm of the villages, which only really seem to come to life during vintage time. How these villages mostly appear so deserted is a piece of French magic. The Frenchman lives behind his house—in every sense of the word, and you will notice that there are no front gardens. The house-owner, when he is not actually away working, possibly in some vineyard quite distant from his home, may be in his cellar or out of sight elsewhere, in whatever building he has by way of a workshop.

The Corton Circuit

The best route to take for this mini-tour follows the old road towards Dijon, going over the autoroute. Immediately, there are vines on either side of the road. To the right is the village of Chorey-lès-Beaune, the wines of which, although enjoying a village *appellation*, are usually used as part of shippers' blends for Côte de Beaune Villages (see page 116). As these wines of Chorey are grown entirely on the plain, they do not claim to have outstanding characteristics, but they are most firm, and ideal for blending as a unifying force with more fragrant wines.

The Corton circuit starts immediately after Chorey, to the left, and a signpost to the village of Aloxe-Corton is clearly marked. This minor road has the appearance of a private drive because it is extremely straight, and, at the end, there comes in sight a most beautiful house, called the Château de Corton, which is now the trading home of a mail-order house, André Frères. The village has many examples of the attractive Burgundian roofs and there is a great deal of warmth about the architecture, and the village reflects this warmth, particularly during the late evening in high summer when the sun's rays are strong and some of the buildings actually seem even more yellow. As the houses in Aloxe include several that were built for merchants, they have a superiority of architecture that is not found in the more workmanlike villages nearby.

Aloxe Corton lies at the foot of the Montagne de Corton and behind the village the ground rises quite steeply, the vineyards climbing upwards towards the wooded, tree-topped hill. The great vineyard, Corton Charlemagne, then extends in a great loop round the hill towards the village of Pernand, but the production of this vineyard, while it actually traverses the boundary of Pernand, is entitled to the Corton Charlemagne *appellation*. The ownership of this vineyard is split between several large owners, of whom Louis Latour and Jaboulet-Vercherre are the best known, as well as other small *vignerons*, who, until recently, would sell their wines to the Beaune shippers but who now, more and more, reserve their stocks for their own bottling and for sale to private customers. The Corton Charlemagne wines are exclusively white, with a style rich in flavour yet fully dry, a description which may appear contradictory, but the sense of their richness can be noticed when they age and their taste becomes all-pervading.

Apart from the Charlemagne, the finest wines from the leading vineyards of Aloxe-Corton are red. Notice should be taken of Le Corton, which produces the most exciting and long-lived bottles of all Côte de Beaune wines. They are rightly described as *vins de garde* (wines to keep) because they do have extraordinary longevity—up to 25 years, if kept in sound cellarage. The immediate flavour of Corton may appear slightly thick and earthy, but time erases the hardness and replaces it with a refinement that is quite classical, and with a style that is extremely close to the finest Côte de Nuits.

The interesting situation of the vineyard Le Corton shows how geographical location and position relating to the sun play such an important part. Le Corton is a long, thin strip of vineyard, beneath the Bois de Corton, where the northern end will enjoy early sunshine and the southern end will see much more of the late and, possibly, drier hours of daylight. There is a curiosity of labelling in Corton in that the *premier cru* vineyards are preceded simply by the word "Corton", and it is only the second growth vineyards that are preceded by the full village title "Aloxe-Corton".

Wines from the following classified vineyards will be regularly available: Le Corton; Clos du Roi; Vigne au Saint; Les Maréchaudes; Les Bressandes.

Growers/*négociants'* labels widely distributed include P.A. André (visitors by appointment); Louis Latour; Prince de Mérode.

Pernand Vergelesses

As the important vineyards sweeping round from the Bois de Corton are entitled to the *appellation* 'Corton', the production of red and white Pernand Vergelesses is limited and the wines are certainly not well known. The reds are big wines, without the grace of Corton or the softness of Savigny, but they are rewarding after some years in bottle, having power and a noticeable *goût de terroir*—a flavour of the particular vineyard soil. An example of this is the excellent vineyard wine *Ile de Vergelesses*, offered by Louis Latour.

White wines under the village name must be produced from the 'Chardonnay' grape, which (see page 17) is the sole white grape for both village and single vineyard wines of the Côte d'Or. There is a distinct similarity between the whites of Pernand and the neighbouring Corton Charlemagne, but they are difficult to find: the *négociant* Marcel Amance, in Santenay, offers an excellent Pernand white in good vintages, which he buys from a grower who also has vines in the Corton Charlemagne vineyard. The other permitted white grape variety, the 'Aligoté', can only be sold under its original *appellation*, but, grown in Pernand, it does produce some of the best qualities. If you are interested in contrasts, then contemplate the modern autoroute A6 from the ancient village of Pernand Vergelesses—the two worlds do not meet.

Wines from the following classified vineyards will be regularly available: Ile de Vergelesses, Les Fichots. Growers'/ *négociants'* labels that are widely distributed are: Dubrueil Père & Fils, Bonneau du Mattray, Rapet Père et Fils. No visits appear to be possible at the time of writing.

Savigny-lès-Beaune

To the visitor arriving via the Autoroute A6 into the Côte d'Or, Savigny is the first village to be seen as the motorway drops down sharply from the plateau towards Beaune. Savigny-lès-Beaune shelters in the valley below on the left, with its main vineyards spreading out from the valley, round the hill up to Pernand Vergelesses, towards the front of Aloxe Corton near the RN74, and down towards Beaune, where the Savigny vineyards abruptly end at the motorway. On this part of the motorway several shippers have built new fermentation cellars, including Chanson Père et Fils, who wished to be nearer to their two exclusive vineyard holdings in the Beaune/Savigny area, as in the past they had logistic problems of fermentation during an abundant harvest: the grapes would begin to ferment en route in the hot weather.

Savigny-lès-Beaune is a pretty village with a very reasonable hotel, l'Ouvrée, which is suitable as a Côte d'Or base. The proprietor, M. Petitjean, owns several plots of vines in Savigny and his wine is naturally sold in the restaurant.

The majority of wines from Savigny-lès-Beaune are red, with a soft and fragrant smell. They can be good if drunk earlier than their more famous neighbours. Savignby is an excellent example of a medium-priced wine as against the often inflated value of more fashionable villages.

A small quantity of white wine is made and, again, the 'Aligoté' of this village is much sought after by the shippers for their blends. Wines from the following classified vineyards will be regularly available: Aux Vergelesses, Marconnets, La Dominode, Aux Guettes and Les Lavières.

Chorey-lès-Beaune and Ladoix-Serrigny

Ladoix-Serrigny is the first, or, as you may wish, the last of the villages of the Côte de Beaune. This double hamlet is entitled to its own village label, but the best sites are allowed the *appellation* Aloxe Corton for the red wines and Corton Charlemagne for the whites. This is a quirk of geography, as these sites are simply an extension of the prime sites of Aloxe Corton, continuing across the east face of the slopes of the Bois de Corton. The ordinary village wine is used for blending as Côte de Beaune Villages.

Growers/*négociants'* labels of Chorey-lés-Beaune that are widely distributed are: Arnoux Père & Fils (visits accepted), J. Germain at the Château de Chorey, and R. Voarick.

Beaune and the Côte de Beaune Routes

In former times, the wines of Beaune were probably synonymous with Burgundy in general, as far as most foreigners were concerned. The Beaune vineyard itself has the greatest 'surface' or area under vines of all the Burgundy region round about, although it does not produce as much wine as, for example, Pommard. But it is easy to understand why the wines became so well known: not only were they within easy reach of the town of Beaune itself, but other named vineyards which are now producing wines under their own labels, such as Pernand and Savigny, probably in the past were all sold as simply 'Beaune'. (In case of confusion, it should be stressed that, in this context, the references to Beaune are solely to the wines, and not to the town, culture, or anything else.)

Although you can make a rapid trip by taking the car in the direction of the Montagne de Beaune and Bouze-lès-Beaune to get a panorama of the vineyards, it may be of interest to know that the excursion into the Beaune vineyards is perfectly practicable on foot, even if you start by walking from Beaune itself. Leave the road and follow the vineyard tracks, wander about for a couple of hours, and you will have a wonderful impression of being among the vines and seeing 'where it all happens' while you walk off any excesses of Burgundian fare and wine that you may have incurred. Remember, it is perfectly permissible to follow vineyard tracks, but don't walk between the rows of vines, and remember to say 'Bonjour' to anyone you meet. The Burgundians will usually be delighted to see you taking an active interest in the vineyard.

In following this itinerary, visitors must expect to see the contrast between modern and old France: from quite near to Beaune itself one can look down on the medieval town, encircled by its ramparts, which, like most French towns today, has in recent years spread out into a sprawl of modern development outside. In the modern part of Beaune, in other words the suburbs, many of the major wine houses now have their installations for bottling and actually making the wine (in the *cuveries* or press houses); it is from these modern installations that about half-a-dozen of the important shippers will do the despatch of their wine. In case anyone should be inclined to despise these modern installations outside the centre of Beaune, it must be stressed that, by moving part of their premises in this way, the shippers have enabled the centre of the town to remain free of juggernaut lorries and great traffic confusion, which the narrow streets cannot cope with.

It is worth reminding the reader that the appellation 'Beaune' is not the same as Côte de Beaune or Côte de Beaune Villages (for these, see page 116). The importance of distinguishing in one's mind between the three names—Beaune, Côte de Beaune and Côte de Beaune Villages—is that in fact they are distant areas and productions in their own right and consequently have separate places in the wine social order.

The actual wines of the *appellation* Beaune are attractive starting wines for the beginner, learning about Burgundy, for they are fullish in style and easy to drink. While there is a tiny amount of white wine, the vast majority of Beaune is red. In tracing the history of the style of wines made from these ancient vineyards, we find a traditional vinification to create wines of a light fruitiness without the same stamina as some of the more lordly villages of the Côte de Nuits.

Records show that Beaune wines were essentially trading wines that became well known in Paris and, later, in London, as representing Burgundy. By the nature of the vineyard's soil and exposed position, it is quite natural for this style and character to be maintained to the present day; but it may be a little unfair, because there are some outstanding wines produced. I would name for preference the tiny vineyard, owned by Bouchard Père et Fils, of the Vigne de l'Enfant Jésus—and there are others. But it is nevertheless possible to postulate the theory that when, after the French Revolution at the end of the eighteenth-century, the domination of the vineyards by the religious establishments and great estates of the aristocracy came to an end, it was the Beaune vineyards that were first purchased by the established shippers in the nineteenth century for more rapid commercialisation, simply because of the quality of wine produced. The name 'Beaune' was easy to sell, and the style of wine was easily drinkable.

When I am faced with a lengthy 'gastronomic' meal, I am always cheered to see the wines of Beaune served, as they blend so well with the richer and more succulent foods and cause no difficulty with digestion: so, oddly enough, the more demanding wines of the Côte d'Or, with their concentrated flavours, can be more easily enjoyed—and talked about—when they accompany somewhat simpler dishes. Beaune wines, to me, have an uninhibited and slightly casual approach and, with the benefit of a few years' sales experience, dealing with the wines of Beaune, I can say that now all these wines are bottled in the region of production, the demand for Beaune has fallen away.

It appears that the majority of regular Burgundy drinkers prefer the greater stamina of Corton, Pommard and Volnay. To redress this balance, I put in a strong plea for people to forget all the nasty Beaunes they may have drunk—Beaunes which were bottled in Britain—and return once more to these charming and most helpful wines. Also, the price is never quite as high as the wines I've mentioned above.

The town of Beaune has been the wine trade centre of the Côte d'Or since the fourteenth century. The region has been variously owned by many different proprietors—the church and sundry religious orders, the aristocrats, the Crown and even the Knights of Malta, until the change of land ownership following the 1789 Revolution, when the proprietors were dispossessed and the vineyards auctioned. The vineyards did not pass down to the real peasant worker, as they were purchased by the small, existing growers and by the merchants. During the nineteenth century and the first half of this century, the shippers gradually acquired more vineyards and, in the immediate Beaune area, they have become the principal owners: for example, Drouhin, Chanson and Bouchard Père et Fils.

Hospices de Beaune wines

The wines referred to and labelled as 'Hospices de Beaune' are those that belong to this institution, which consists of the Hôtel-Dieu de Beaune and the Hospice de la Charité, also in the town. In 1443, the Chancellor of Burgundy, Nicolas Rolin, and his wife, Guigone de Salins, endowed the Hospices, and their statues may be seen in the courtyard. Rolin was responsible for many of the great architectural glories of Burgundy, and the curious and richly decorated Hôtel-Dieu was built with the aid of Flemish craftsmen, which accounts for its unusual style. The Dames Hospitalières, a Flemish nursing order, still staff the institution, but accommodation is now in more modern buildings.

The wines are:
WHITE

Cuvée	*Village*	*Vineyard*
Francois de Salins	Corton	Charlemagne
Bahezre de Lanlay	Meursault	Charmes
Loppin	Meursault	
Baudot	Meursault	Genevrières
Philippe le Bon	Meursault	Genevrières

Humblot	Meursault	Poruzot
Goureau	Meursault	Poruzot
Albert Grivault	Meursault	Charmes

RED

Charlotte Dumay	Corton	
Docteur Peste	Corton	
Rameau-Lamarosse	Pernand Vergelesses	Basses Vergelesses
Arthur Girard	Savigny	Marconnet
Forneret	Savigny	Vergelesses, Gravains
Fouquerand	Savigny	Vergelesses, Gravains
Hugues et Louis Betault	Beaune	Grèves, Aigrot
Maurice Drouhin	Beaune	Avaux, Bourcherottes Champimonts, Greves
Dames Hospitalières	Beaune	Bressandes, Mignotte
Nicholas Rolin	Beaune	Centvignes, Greves
Brunet	Beaune	Bressandes, Mignotte
Guigone de Salins	Beaune	Bressandes, Champimonts
Rousseau-Deslandes	Beaune	Centvignes, Montremenots
Dames de la Charité	Pommard	Épenots, Puginens
Billardet	Pommard	Épenots, Noizons
Blondeau	Volnay	Champans, Taille-Pieds
Général Muteau	Volnay	Village, Carelle
Gauvin	Volnay	Santenots
Jehan de Massol	Volnay	Santenots
Lebelin	Monthelie	Duresses
Boillot	Auxey-Duresses	Duresses

Visiting the Hôtel-Dieu

Guided tours take visitors round the Hôtel-Dieu, and about an hour should be allowed for this. You should particularly appreciate the remarkably patterned roof, the Salle des Pauvres, with the curtained bunk-type beds so arranged that the patients could see the celebration of Mass at the end of the huge room, also the pharmacy, the enormous kitchen, and the great work of art, Roger van der Weiden's *Last Judgment*.

The benefactors of the Hôtel-Dieu and Hospice de la Charité endowed these institutions with vineyards, and it became an established tradition for these wines to bear the names of the original owners. All the wines come from the Côte de Beaune and, since 1859, they have been sold at a public auction in all but exceptionally bad years. The auctions attract great publicity and buyers from all over the world, and the Trois Glorieuses (see pages 9–11), during the third weekend in November, coincide with them.

Today, the *cuvées* or vattings of the wines sold at the Hospices de Beaune are twenty-four of red and nine of white, plus some brandies and *marc* (see page 34). They range from Meursault in the south of the region to Corton in the north.

The Hospices labels tell the village from which the wine comes, the vineyard, and the *cuvée* (vatting). In some instances, wines from two or three vineyards in the same village may be blended together to make up a *cuvée,* and when this happens the wine will bear the A.C. of the village. The *cuvée,* as has been said, bears the name of the original benefactor, donor of either the plot of vineyard or a particular vatting and, usually, this name of an individual is as well known as the A.C.

THE SALE

The Hospices are no longer solely financed by the sale of wines, the cost of modern medicine now exceeding even the most expensive of these, but the vineyards do contribute substantially to their upkeep. Until recent years, the prices fetched at the Hospices auction were a strong indication of market prices of Burgundy in general, but since 1970, with the inflationary spiral of fine wines, the Hospices wines have tended to surpass in price the maximum that shippers find that they are able to obtain for wines bearing same A.C.s. Those who understandably, think of Beaune wines as red wines, should remember that it is usually a white wine, Corton Charlemagne Cuvée François de Salins, that fetches the highest price.

The wines are offered at auction in lots of casks (*pièces*), the Burgundian cask of oak, which contains approximately 300 bottles or 220 litres. In the 1975 sale, 267 *pièces* were listed, the sizes of the separate lots varying between five and nine *pièces* per lot. Buyers have to remove the *pièces* from the Hospices' cellars within one month of the sale, and henceforth the bottling of the contents of the casks becomes the sole responsibility of the purchaser. It will, therefore, be appreciated that wines from the same vineyards and indeed from the same named *cuvée* may vary considerably, according to who does the bottling. It is therefore as unwise to make generalisations about the Hospices wines as it is to generalise about Burgundy: the ultimate quality and style can only be determined by whoever buys the wine.

It is worth stressing that, although the visitor may find much of interest to see in Beaune at the time of the sale, admission to the auction is by ticket only and, because space is limited, places are taken by the wine trade and their guests. Accommodation is very difficult to find at sale time and all

Mounting casks (pièces) for storage

restaurants and shops are crowded, so that it is unwise to count
on seeing the auction or staying in Beaune in late November.

Pommard

A visit here can extend the tour of the Beaune vineyards or, if
you have sufficient time, make a pleasant tour on its own. Leave
the boulevard or circling road around Beaune and aim south,
on the RN74. Soon after the Samotel (where you can stay and
have a vineyard view from your window), take the right-hand
road in the fork, N73, signposted 'Autun'; this leads directly to
Pommard itself. As you turn off at this junction, the Pommard
vineyards are on the left and right of the road. Ahead, take the
way through a chain of villages with names that mean much to
the lover of wine—Volnay, Monthélie, Auxey Duresses, Saint
Romain. You can return later by the road that leads off from
Monthélie to Meursault, through Puligny Montrachet,
Chassage Montrachet and as far as Santenay, from which point
you can return to Beaune via Chagny on the RN74. Just before
you reach Pommard itself, on rising ground to the right, note
the vineyard of Les Epenots (or Epenaux—the spelling can
vary). On the left here is the fine-looking Château de Pommard, a single enclosed vineyard, a rarity in Burgundy, owned
by M. Laplanche. Visitors can be received here.

Pommard itself is a quiet little wine village; it lives by and,
literally, on wine, every house being that of a *vigneron* or small
proprietor, with cellars beneath the dwellings. Walk about the
little streets and observe the unusual-shaped belfry on the
church. Pommard gets its name from Pomona, the presiding
Roman deity of gardens and fruits (hence the word
pomme = apple), and the wine was a favourite of the great
nineteenth-century author, Victor Hugo. Look out over the
vineyards: the important site, Les Rugiens, often seen on

British wine lists, is on the slightly higher ground between Pommard and its neighbour, Volnay. Turn right in the centre of the village and you can get to the equally famous Clos de la Commaraine vineyard, now owned by the well-known shipper, Jaboulet-Vercherre.

Pommard at its best is a fine wine, with a deep, brilliant colour, a very gracious fruitiness and a softness that develops charmingly as the wine ages; fine Pommard of a great year can be a tremendous wine, but it is not all that easy to find these days. Indeed, Pommard's reputation has, in the opinion of many Europeans, suffered as the result of the enormous popularity of its wines in North America; this market has been prepared to pay prices higher than those of any other export markets in order to get the wine it finds so acceptable. In consequence, not merely does the U.S. buyer now risk not always getting a wine of quality in accordance with the high price paid, but the demand for this wine—it has a name easy for Anglo-Saxons to say with assurance, another factor of by no means negligible importance—has tempted some vignerons to cash in on this popularity. There has therefore been some forcing of production up to the maximum permitted by the A.C. regulations: in other words, the vineyards have been strained so as to make as much wine (and to produce as much money) as can possibly be legally achieved. This has naturally led to a lowering of quality standards. So choose your source of Pommard with especial care!

Wines from the following classified vineyards are usually readily available:

Château de Pommard	Les Pézerolles
Clos de la Commaraine	Clos Micot
Les Épenots (Epeneaux)	Les Arvelets
Les Rugiens	

Growers and négociants whose labels will be featured on many export lists include Jaboulet-Vercherre, Château de Pommard, and Comte Armand.

Volnay

After you leave Pommard, the road climbs somewhat to Volnay and then runs in front of the village. The larger proportion of vineyards is on the left at this stage, so that there is a sensational view of them down to the main road, RN74. In fact, Volnay is an excellent place to stop, to look and to reflect—preferably when you have recently enjoyed a fine bottle of its wine. Survey the vineyards, whether you do so on a sunny day or when the clouds huddle over the Côte d'Or and showers make you glad to be able to get back into the car. Those of us who enjoy wine for its essential simplicity—the pleasure it immediately gives—will claim the enjoyment of fine Burgundy as a stimulus to the tired intellect; we are gratefully drawn into the study of this wonderful wine. So pause on the Volnay road, look back to Pommard, follow the vineyard round and, eventually, go on to Meursault. Wine lovers are very fortunate. Even if you have not always felt this, you will do so when you stop for a moment's thought and silent expression of gratitude in the midst of the birthplaces of so many wonderful wines.

Because it stands a little high, Volnay is exposed to the elements and there is a real danger of frost. This can sometimes be counteracted by heating pots, and placing them strategically among the vines. The pots are filled with charcoal, and lit when the temperature drops to danger point; they send out a general warmth in their vicinity, so that the frost cannot bite and destroy the vegetation.

Perhaps because of this exposure, the wines of Volnay are markedly delicate and sometimes even fragile: but observe the subtle flavours of good Volnay too, underlying the delicacy. Take time. Let the Volnay breathe and develop in the glass—swing the wine round a little to encourage this, and then concentrate on the wine as you drink it. Volnays are good 'beginners' wines', because they do please immediately, with their soft, but insinuating bouquet and light fruitiness that leads on to a deeper velvetiness and lasting charm.

Volnay wines are red, yet there is an odd contradiction in the A.C. laws concerning the white wines which are also grown there, for these, adjacent to Meursault as they are, are entitled to the A.C. Meursault and not Volnay. In the same bureaucratic way, the best red wines that are the product of vineyards inside the meursault defined area are entitled to the label Volnay-Santenots or, if of a slightly lower quality, the label may bear the straight name Volnay.

Wines from the following vineyards are usually widely available:

Clos des Angles	Fremiets
Caillerets	Pousse d'Or
Champans	Santenots (in Meursault)
Clos des Chênes	Chevrets

Growers and négociants whose labels are widely distributed include:

Domaine de la Pousse d'Or	Bouchard Père & Fils
Henri Boillot	Le Cellier Volnaysien
Bernard Delagrange	Marquis d'Angerville

Monthélie

After leaving Volnay, the road forks: the left-hand route goes to Meursault and the right-hand to Monthélie, Auxey Duresses and Saint Romain. Allow about 45 minutes if you are going to see Monthélie and the other villages, or, if you haven't time, go straight to Meursault. Monthélie is a tiny, ancient village, tucked around the corner of the hill on high ground. It is said to get more sun than any other village of the Côte d'Or, and it is naturally sheltered. But the soil is very poor indeed—no other crop except vines can be successfully grown. Note, too, the 'quilted' effect produced by the overlapping tiles, with their scalloped edges, on the roofs of the houses—these are true 'old Burgundy'.

Monthélie's wines are 97 per cent red, and the white is a rarity, although it is made. Formerly the wines of Monthélie would be used for the *cuvées* (vattings) of Volnay and even of Pommard when these wines, on account of their names, were the big-selling Burgundies. But Monthélie got its own *appellation* in 1937 and since then has been making strenuous efforts to get its wines known and estimated in their own right. They are generally light in style and very fragrant, with a clear, brilliant red colour—and are, of course, usually less expensive than other Côte de Beaune wines. Monthélie is also able to be drunk and enjoyed when, by wine standards, it is still quite young: some Monthélies are delicious as early as three or four years after their vintages. The white wines, which are never seen on export lists, should certainly be sampled in the village café.

Monthélie is now becoming widely available on wine lists and the wines of the classified vineyard, Les Champs-Fulliot, can sometimes also be found.

The growers' cooperative can receive visitors to their premises, Les Caves de Monthélie, from Easter until November. Robert & Bernard de Suremain, at the Château de Monthélie, can also receive visitors, and even coach parties if an appointment is made at Les Caves de Monthélie.

Auxey Duresses

Continuing along the right-hand fork past Monthélie, the next village, Auxey Duresses, is set in the entrance to a gorge dominated by the Mont Meliam; the principal vineyards lie to the right, on ground that is too high to produce great wines. A vineyard that is too exposed will suffer more from variations in the weather than one that is slightly sheltered. Hence the finest growths come from sites that are half or two-thirds up a slope, the rising ground behind them both offering some protection and providing drainage to feed them.

A parenthesis on pronunciation here: you will find Burgundians in the countryside pronouncing the 'x' of their villages as a true 'x' sound. But at school they—and everyone else—will be instructed to pronounce the 'x' as a double 's'. The village names to which this applies in the Côte d'Or are Fixin, Aloxe Corton and Auxey Duresses, and Buxy in the Côte Chalonnaise. So, when you use these names you have to decide whether you want to use 'French' pronunciation and say 'Fissin', or to opt for the clearer Burgundian.

Auxey Duresses produces around 70 per cent red and 30 per cent white wine. Both of these can now be found on the British market; they represent real value and have not so far had their prices inflated by fashion. The red is not appreciably different from Monthélie—in other words, it is a small-scale Volnay. The white wines are capable of rivalling those of Meursault, without quite developing the depth of flavour that is associated with this famous name. The white wines give an agreeable feel of power and their bouquet is delightful, but I recommend that you select young vintages because these wines have a tendency to maderise or discolour quickly, and therefore their peak point is comparatively short.

The wines and the gastronomy of the region can be sampled, without an undue deficit to the pocket, at La Crémaillère in Auxey Duresses.

Wines will usually be available from the classified vineyards of: Les Duresses, Clos du Moulin des Moines, and special mention should also be made of the Cuvée Boillot, of the Hospices de Beaune, which is usually an excellent red wine.

Growers: *négociants* whose labels are widely distributed are: J. Leroy (co-distributor of the Domaine de la Romanée Conti), and Michel Prunier.

The Caveau Communal in Auxey may be visited if an appointment is previously made.

Saint Romain

The last village of this wine route through the Côte de Beaune received its full appellation as recently as 1967. Since then, the grower Roland Thévenin has promoted the wines to great effect. (He is also an important grower in Puligny Montrachet.)

The vineyards of St. Romain are the highest of the whole Côte d'Or. On this exposed position, the 'Chardonnay' grape, producing white wine, is more hardy than the 'Pinot Noir' for the reds. When drunk young and fresh, St. Romain Blanc is an excellent, fresh apéritif wine; the red wine can be an ideal prelude to something greater. The growers: *négociants* whose labels are widely distributed are: Roland Thévenin, and Chanson, the Beaune shippers, who also promote this *appellation*.

There are no individual vineyards worth recording in this area but, because of St. Romain's position, it is worth stopping and walking up to the panoramic lookout on the summit of the mountain, which is reached by a path on the right, past farm buildings. On a clear day, it is possible to see over the Mâconnais and Beaujolais to the south and, eastwards, across the Saône Valley to the Alps.

If you follow the RN73 out of Auxey Duresses, the road climbs on to the Hautes Côtes de Beaune towards Nolay and

Autun. Travelling by this route, there is a country road which reaches Santenay at the far end of the Côtes de Beaune, via Nolay and Paris L'Hôpital, crossing over the RN6 (the old Lyon–Paris road). If there is time to spare on this excursion, detours should certainly be made to see the still impressive establishment of Cluny (much smaller than in its great days) and the superb Romanesque cathedral at Autun.

Meursault and La Côte des Blancs

Starting at the road fork outside Volnay, the left-hand road runs down into Meursault, which can also be reached from the main RN74. This is perhaps an essential trip for anyone hoping to learn about white Burgundy.

Meursault is not a village, but it is also not quite a town. However, it is the capital of La Côte de Blancs, which, besides Meursault, includes the villages of Blagny, Puligny Montrachet and Chassagne Montrachet. From these villages come the finest dry white wines in the world. The atmosphere of the place, evocative of dry white wines, is strongest in Meursault. The straggly narrow streets are abundantly adorned with growers' signs, and cellars are obviously almost everywhere under your feet. It is a romantic capital, with a little square around the fourteenth-century St. Nicolas church with its elegant spire (a mini-model of the cathedral at Autun). Opposite the church is the Restaurant Mère Daugier, which specialises in hot pâté! If you stay there, however, remember to ask for a room at the rear, for at the front you will be nearer to the church bells than is good for the ears. Meursault is also well organised for camping sites and provides for the devotees of motels.

Part of the festivities of the Hospices de Beaune auction weekend (pages 9–11) take place in Meursault. The luncheon on the last day is called La Paulée.

The ruins of the twelfth-century Hôpital de Meursault sit on the other side of the main road (RN74) at the junction where it meets the village road. This building was originally a lepers' hospital and hence was outside the town, but many years ago it fell into disuse, although it is still a handsome ruin. Notice the original level of the entrance to the hospital, which is now several feet below the main road—an example of how some buildings can sink and roads be built up.

Meursault is known uniquely for white wines, as previously mentioned. The small amount of red wine that is grown on the Volnay boundary is entitled to the Volnay *appellation.*

Within the Meursault *appellation* area are included some of the wines from the hamlet of Blagny, that sits higher up the slope between Meursault and Puligny. The adjectives used by generations of wine writers to indicate the flavour of Meursault have perhaps helped towards the belief in the alleged pomposity of the wine trade, but it really is difficult to describe such a complex family of wines.

Meursault is distinctive in bouquet, combining the smell of light fruit and developing traces of nuttiness as it ages. Its colour starts life quite pale, almost a pale lemon tone, but this changes soon to a full, definite yellow. The taste contrasts richness with an essential dryness; balance between these two is essential for fine Meursault, which is the fullest and most rounded of all the Côte d'Or white wines. What Meursault may sometimes lack is the class and refinement of the wines that come from the great Puligny vineyards (page 71). The best wines of Meursault will last five or six years, but do not be tempted to keep it for too long, as there is nothing worse than old white Burgundy, in my view—its greatness as a superb white wine lies in the combination of freshness and maturity.

Between the two of Meursault and the boundary of Puligny, there are five vineyards of international repute. It would be reasonable, therefore, to suppose that, as each of these vineyards produces wines that are different in shades of character, it should be possible to offer individual tasting notes about each of them. But, as will have been appreciated by the reader who has understood the complexity of Burgundy wines, there are no single proprietors of these vineyards, and therefore each owner will make a wine slightly different from that of his neighbour: he will pick the grapes at a different time, he may vinify in a slightly individual way; he—or the shipper who buys from him—will handle the wines according to the 'style of the house'. So, in the end, it really is impossible to make the sort of generalisations that enable the student of wine to put a definite tag on wines such as these.

It might, nevertheless, be of some slight help if basic characteristics are mentioned. The vineyard Goutte d'Or will usually possess the fullest character, contrary to Les Charmes, where bouquet and fruity balance linger more gently. Les Perrières and Poruzots have more aggressive style, leaving the vineyard of Les Generières to unite all these charming subtleties. But it's also fair to say that I could probably find exceptions to all these descriptions in the cellars of any Meursault shipper at any time.

Wines from the following classified vineyards will be regularly available: Perrières, Charmes, Genevrières, Poruzots, Goutte d'Or and Chevalières.

Visits can be made to Château de Meursault (now owned by Patriarche Père & Fils of Beaune) and there are tastings in the fourteenth-century cellars. There are daily tastings (except Fridays) at Maison de Meursault (a growers' co-operative), and tastings, too, at Le Manoir Murisaltien.

The following growers can receive visits if an appointment is made:

Jean Ampeau Germain   Jean Monnier

Raymond Javillier   Domaine Prieur
Domaine Comte Lafond   Ropiteau Frères

Puligny Montrachet

There is a vineyard circuit road linking Meursault with Puligny without re-joining the main road, from which it is evident that the vines of both villages are separated only by tracks. En route, you see Blagny to the right; its wines are divided between Meursault and Puligny Montrachet, but the village name is attached, such as Meursault-Blagny or Puligny-Montrachet-Blagny. A small amount of red wine is produced and is just named Blagny.

Puligny, when seen in the sun, has a sense of retained heat and strength; it is often apparently empty of people, but they are there somewhere. They produce, within this vineyard's limits, the greatest selection of dry white wines in the world. Taking the road signposted 'Chassagne Montrachet and Santenay', you gently climb out of the village, passing vineyards on the left and right, up towards the sites of Les Bienvenues, Bâtard Montrachet, Le Montrachet and Chevalier Montrachet. These great vineyards follow each other up the hill, divided only by the Chassagne road, which turns sharply left between Bâtard Montrachet and Le Montrachet. The latter is on the right: both have walled enclosures and doorways into the vineyard. Here is an essential stopping point from which to feast the eyes and senses on the glorious view. Looking back towards Meursault down a track road, you will see other great vineyards of Puligny—Les Caillerets, Les Folatières, Clos de la Garenne and Champ Canet on middle ground to the left and, easing down towards the village, Les Pucelles, Calvoillon, Les Referts and Les Combettes. So all the great white wines are produced on this gentle hillside in a long line, but varying in their position to the sun and the changes of soil substance, which will affect and alter the final wines in a subtle range of ways. Le Montrachet and Bâtard Montrachet straddle the boundary with Chassagne, but these vineyards have their own *appellation*, so there is no question of having to determine whether the wine is produced in Puligny or Chassagne.

Le Montrachet is unique—the concentration of fruit and acidity produces flavours of exquisite refinement, capable of living beyond reasonable age, as white wines are usually rated. In 1975, a Grand Montrachet 1929 of Baron Thénard was found to be a perfect old gentleman—polite, stimulated by company, but quickly tired. Please forgive the emotional language: it is not intended pomposity, but passion. I shall never forget that bottle!

Sufficient homage having been paid to Le Montrachet, the road descends to the RN6, the old Lyon-Paris highway before the Autoroute A6 existed. In fact, the last vineyard on the left before the RN6 is Criots Bâtard Montrachet (tiny, approximately 2 hectares in extent) where the whole vineyard lies within Chassagne and is consequently separated from the village and the rest of Chassagne vineyards by the main road. I have noticed that Criots Bâtard Montrachet does not age as graciously as the Chevalier, Bâtard, Bienvenues and Le Montrachet, and it would drink at its best some three or four years after the vintage, but in the rare examples that are to be found the bouquet is dramatic in its power, smelling faintly of lemon. The after-flavours of these great vineyards will last within the mouth after the last drop has vanished down the throat.

Wines from the following classified vineyards will be regularly available:

Le Montrachet	Les Chalumeaux
Bâtard Montrachet	Les Caillerets (formerly called
Chevalier Montrachet	Les Demoiselles)
Bienvenues-Bâtard-	Les Folatières
Montrachet	Clavoillon
Les Combettes	
Les Pucelles	

The following growers' labels are widely distributed:

Domaine Leflaive	Jean Pascal
Henri Clare	Domaine Sauzet
Dupard Aîné	Jean Chartron

The majority of Puligny Montrachet village wines and even single vineyard wines will be found under *négociants'* labels. Prices are very high, placing them well above the normal level to be afforded in the U.K. for all but special occasion drinking.

Chassagne Montrachet

Some additional sorting out of the wine names may be helpful here. Because, on wine lists, the top and most highly priced white Burgundy is Le Montrachet in many instances, then its associates, such as Chevalier, Bâtard and Bienvenues-Bâtard, followed by the village wine of Puligny-Montrachet, it has been assumed, by inference, that the wines of Chassagne-Montrachet are white wines only. This view has only been corrected in recent years by the wider introduction on to merchants' lists of the really excellent red wine from Chassagne Montrachet.

Historically, Chassagne Montrachet has always produced more red wine than white. The proportions now are 60 per cent red, as against 40 per cent white. Past descriptions of the qualities of red Chassagne draw attention to the fact that the best Chassagne is more similar in character to the wines of the Côte de Nuits than to those of the Côte de Beaune, to which it belongs. The reason for this praise lies in the ability of Chassagne to produce dark, fattish wines, with a smoothness developing with age. For example, there is a group of vineyards at the southern end of Chassagne, immediately bordering on Santenay, which are entitled to add 'Morgeot' after the village name. This may also be done with the white wines, where several growers are regularly vinifying most distinguished qualities of wines. The Domaine Duc de Magenta owns a small plot, the Clos de la Chapelle, which is within the vineyard L'Abbaye de Morgeot, where the finest wines are produced; the 1972 vintage is a wonder. The village white wines of Chassagne Montrachet can happily be compared with those of Meursault and Puligny during their youth, but some lose their refinement when allowed to remain in bottle too long.

Wines from the following will be regularly available:

Le Montrachet (white)	La Maltroie (red and white)
Bâtard Montrachet (white)	Les Grandes Ruchottes (white)
Criots Bâtard Montrachet (white)	Les Ruchottes (white)
	Clos St. Jean (red and white)
L'Abbaye de Morgeot (red and white)	Les Bourdriottes (red and white)
Morgeot (red and white)	

The following growers' labels are widely distributed:

Jean Bachetet	Marquis de Laguiche
Edmond Delagrange	Albert Morey
Domaine Duc de Magenta	Ramonet-Prudhon
Jacques Gagnard Delagrange	Bachelet-Ramonet

Amongst the *négociants*, Ponnelle, Amance, Audiffred, Drouhin always have a typical and representative village wine.

St. Aubin

If, when you reach the RN6 to cross over from the great Montrachet vineyards into Chassagne village, you turn right in to the main road, up the hill on the right are two villages, Gamay and St. Aubin. Both produce red and white wines of pleasant qualities, yet never truly great because the vineyards, being on high ground, are exposed to the worst elements of the weather. The red wines are often used for blending into wines labelled Côte de Beaune Villages; the white wines, produced from the more hardy Chardonnay, are really worth trying as the village is now ably promoted by some young growers who are introducing improved methods of viticulture and vinification. It is very rare to see St. Aubin wines offered under vineyard names.

Two growers: *négociants'* labels are widely distributed: Jean Lamy et ses Fils, and Roux Père et Fils.

Santenay

To me there is a special reason for this village to receive more coverage than perhaps its viticultural status deserves. In 1934, Constable's Wine Library published *Burgundy*, by Stephen Gwyn. In this book, Gwyn acknowledges his intense educational friendship with M. Prosper Maufoux of Santenay, describing him as being very special in his vocation as a *négociant-éleveur*. This term means that M. Maufoux does not grow wines himself but buys from the grower after the vintage and subsequent fermentation, then keeping the wines during their time in wood before the bottling. Maufoux's grandson, Pierre, now directs the family business. He has inherited the same dedication to honesty and integrity—qualities that are precious in Burgundy when dealing with a complex and sometimes tempting commercial prospect.

Prosper Maufoux as a firm have been represented in Great Britain for many years by Deinhard & Company, the famous German wine shippers. When my colleagues and I sought to establish our own direct buying arrangements for the firm of Laytons, we were kindly allowed by Pierre Maufoux to re-establish with him the shipping firm Marcel Amance et Cie. This name commemorates Marcel Maufoux, who was killed during the First World War in the area of Amance in the Argonne, after being decorated for valour on the battlefield. So I am linked in several ways, personal and commercial, with Santenay.

For Gwyn, Santenay was his Burgundy 'home', and for me it is good fortune to follow Gwyn as a visitor and merchant to the Maufoux family. Too many people are cynical about Burgundy wines and, unfortunately, it is easy to taste the evidence of poor wines that hide behind famous *appellations*. But when you speak with Pierre Maufoux you have faith—and it must be said that I am a businessman as well as a lover of good wine, so that I need convincing commercially as well as personally.

Santenay is a large village split into two portions—Haut Santenay and Bas Santenay—but it is more accurately called Santenay-les-Bains, as the Source Carnot offers the most lithuated water in Europe, reputedly beneficial for gout and rheumatism. Nearby is a home for retired railwaymen, and, close to the village, the Casino de Santenay—a strangely off-beat gambling house, full at weekends of factory workers from Le Creusot, but empty during the week. The only architectural interest in the village is the Eglise St. Jean, with some fine statues from the twelfth- and seventeeth-centuries.

The road from Chassagne Montrachet will bring you past the major vineyards of Santenay. Here you will notice the very recent replanting of vines further up the hill, on land formerly left for scrubland when labour became difficult to obtain because of the hard physical work involved on high ground. These plantations will be yielding wines of quality sufficient to warrant exporting within a few years.

For the visitor who can spare some minutes for an uphill walk to view the landscape that includes vines, many wild flowers, and the two villages of Santenay, I recommend taking the path leading off the main square where the Chassagne road enters the villages out into the vines (just ask anyone you meet, and he will point to the path). On this hill above Santenay there is a fine stone memorial, sculpted by David Norris, placed as a tribute to three of my colleagues killed in the Paris air disaster of March 1974—they loved Burgundy and knew it well. It is a magnificent position and the climb will never be regretted.

Santenay is a red wine village, making just a tiny quantity of white wine. It is the last notable village of the Côte de Beaune and the lie of the land alters the direction in which the vines are planted from facing south-east in Chassagne to due south in Santenay. This enables the vines to get the maximum exposure to the sun. Look at the lines in which they are planted, and you will see what I mean.

The red wines are a bit of a mixture. They can be found light and fruity, but there are still a few growers with old vines, who produce dark, earthy, heavyweights. The former styles tend to be bottled by the growers, the latter to be purchased by *négociants* for the export market, where wines need to stand up to varying storage and climatic conditions, and where this heavier style can be synonymous with robustness. Santenay does not produce wines of great stamina, so it is advisable to drink them within six or seven years. The rare white wines are usually very similar to those of Chassagne Montrachet.

Wines from the following classified vineyards will be usually available:

Les Gravières	Le Passe-Temps
Clos de Tavannes	

Growers/*négociants*' labels that are widely distributed:

Prosper Maufoux	Ph. Chapelle et
Marcel Amance	Fils-Domaine des
(both the above arrange	Hautes Cornières
visits by appointment)	René Fleurot
Joseph Belland	G. Prieur

Dezize-lès-Maranges, Cheilly-lès-Maranges, Sampigny-lès-Maranges

These three rather broken-down villages are the official end of the Côte de Beaune, but are all situated round the hill from Santenay. Whilst each village has its own *appellation*, my enquiries show that the wines are mostly purchased by *négociants* for their Côte de Beaune Villages blends.

La Côte de Nuits

Many readers of this book will already possess a fair knowledge of wine. But there will also be others who, for the first time, are developing an interest in it, as well as some who know a little about Burgundy already, and who are trying to deepen their knowledge. As there is always more to be learned, for every one of us, when we tackle wine, I am going to re-state certain basics which I think will be of help to visitors who, perhaps for the first time, are in a region where great classic wines are made and who want to find out a bit more about them.

First, it is important to be clear in your mind about what may be called the geographical skeleton of the Burgundy wine area. This really will add to your future enjoyment of the wines made within it. So, study the map (page 46) and this part of the book will not seem difficult.

The Côte de Nuits has a romantic-sounding name and so have the most famous village names within its boundaries. At the southern end, the Côte de Nuits connects with the Côte de Beaune at Corgoloin; at its northern boundary there is the village of Fixin. Between these two limits lie the world's most famous and valuable vineyards—although a partisan of Bordeaux might challenge this statement. This Côte is a concentrated, narrow strip of land, about twelve miles in length, running almost due north–south, with the vineyards planted on rising ground up the hillside and finishing only when the soil gives way to the wooded hilltops. The vines face south-east, and from this position they receive the sunshine which continues from early morning into the early evening without burning the grapes. The Côte (the word means 'hillside') includes a succession of villages between which there are many coombs and crevices. These break up the vineyards with changes of soil that are quite noticeable to the eye. Vines that are planted on the flat (reddish clay) by the road (RN74) contrast with those that are planted higher up the hillsides, where pebbles and stones predominate in the topsoil.

The visual difference between the Côte de Nuits and the Côte de Beaune is appreciable because the hillside of the former is closer to the road and much steeper. You have only to stop and look to notice its character.

The wines are almost entirely red. They have certain common characteristics that are probably easier to distinguish when the wine you taste is named to you. Then you can make at least a mental note and try to remember them. This is not an area where 'blind' tasting is very profitable for the student—it is in no way comparable to the way this can be done when tasting red Bordeaux blind.

Not all Côte de Nuits wines are great and fine. This is impossible from a mere 1,600 hectares of vines, with several hundred growers all responsible for vinification—certainly within the relevant laws, but which allow much individuality to owners and makers.

It would not be fair to continue this fulsome praise of Côte de Nuits wines without indicating certain anxieties that are now spreading through the wine trade. The total production of Côte de Nuits wines is much smaller than the Côte de Beaune, resulting in a situation of demand quite often exceeding supply. When the *vignerons'* products are easy to sell, there is a natural decline in attention to detail, and this has begun to show in recent vintages. This may be largely due to the rapid increase in tourism, bringing many willing buyers into direct contact with the producer. It is now estimated that 30 per cent of all Côte de Nuits wines are sold by the grower direct to the consumer. Inevitably there has been some aggravation caused by this new trend, and I must strongly dissuade anyone who may wish to join this buying craze. Leave this job to your merchant!

It is also alleged that Côte de Nuits are beginning to suffer from over-fertilisation of the vineyards to force up production. My experience is not extensive enough to assess the truth of this particular anxiety. However, colour in these wines does seem to be lessening. Too many are lacking in body and, often, they do not have the rich generosity characteristic of the exceptional finesse found in the best wines. Nevertheless, I hope readers will find many Côte de Nuits wines which exemplify why they have gained their reputation. Note the expansive bouquet, the elegance of the fruity flavours and the depth of taste that fills the mouth.

ITINERARY

It is possible to start a Côte de Nuits tour from either Beaune or Dijon, but most of you will probably start from the Beaune area, so I shall assume the journey from south to north.

The actual boundary of the Côte de Nuits is clearly marked at Corgoloin, an ugly village, which is the home of famous marble quarries that, with their neighbour at Comblanchien, spread a thin white film of dust over everything in the vicinity. However, the country route through Pernand Vergelesses and over to Hautes Côtes de Nuits is very pleasant. Follow the signs to Nuits St. Georges. On this route, you emerge through the trees high above Nuits St. Georges and the quarries are by-passed. Between the quarries and Nuits St. Georges (RN74) the wine interest begins at Prémeaux. This is a mere village, but the wines are entitled to be called Nuits St. Georges.

If you go to Nuits St. Georges on the main Beaune-Dijon road (thereby saving a little time), notice the vineyards to the left. Virtually all the village and vineyard appellations will be on the left-hand side going north, as the RN74 is an ancient route originally laid to mark the limit of the fine wines from the hillside. To the right there are many vines extending towards the River Saône and the railway line—but, with rare exceptions, they will be allowed only generic A.C.s.

Nuits St. Georges is the main town and commercial centre of the Côte de Nuits, home of many *commissionnaires* and location of the cellars of several well-known shippers. The most important vineyards in Nuits St. Georges lie to the south of the town, adjacent to the main road between Nuits and the village of Prémeaux.

It is important to remember that the name 'Nuits St. Georges' was until very recently the most abused Côte d'Or label on the U.K. market. Before any control was seriously established, it was perfectly possible for British shippers to buy wines in the 'style' of Nuits St. Georges which, when bottled in England, carried the Nuits St. Georges label. Unfortunately the only arbiter of taste was the shipper. There has always been an expression among British consumers—'Trust your shipper'. This was obviously required with no external control.

There were many shippers whose Nuits St. Georges wines were both genuine and of high quality. But inevitably there were others whose wines were neither. Fortunately times have now changed, with all reputable companies respecting the French law; those that do not may find themselves defending their wines and practices before the courts.

The character of true and genuine Nuits St. Georges is typified by firmness and depth of flavour. It is usually better for keeping. Perhaps the wines of Nuits lack the noble finesse and breeding so obvious in their immediate neighbours to the north, but many excellent, medium-priced wines can be found and enjoyed.

The *appellation* area of Nuits St. Georges covers 375 hectares. It is the effective beginning of the Côte de Nuits, although further down the road the smaller villages of Prissey, Comblanchien and Corgoloin join with Brochon and Fixin to make the wine for the Côte de Nuits Villages labels.

The town of Nuits (St. Georges was added in 1892) should be visited for the fine church of St. Symphorien and the Roman remains to the east of the town at Les Bolards. The road through Nuits is always busy and quite narrow, with shippers' establishments close to the pavement. So, park the car and walk through the side streets leading off the square; the change of atmosphere will mark the amazing tranquillity and timelessness that is so much the essence of the Côte d'Or.

The enthusiastic amateur of wine travelling through the Côte d'Or has opportunities of tasting in each village where facilities are available, but do beware of roadside *dégustations* aimed solely at selling, for only rarely will quality or value be available here. The local restaurants offer a reasonable selection from the Côte d'Or, but prices are expensive for British visitors and vintages will appear young. In the region, the youth of the wine may not detract from the enjoyment, but the bottle age essential for full and mature enjoyment will not have taken place. However, some of the simple regional appellations will often surprise visitors by their quality and they need not be costly.

Wines from the following classified vineyards will be regularly available: Les Procès, Les Pruliers, Les Porrets, Les Vaucrains, Les St. Georges, Les Perdrix, Clos des Corvées, Clos de la Maréchale. And the following growers/*négociants*' labels are widely distributed: J. C. Boisset, Cruse, F. Chauvenet, J. Faiveley, Geisweiler, Domaine Gouges, Grivelet Cusset, Laboure-Roi, Liger Belair, Lupé Cholet, Morin, Jules Bélin (at Prémeaux), Charles Viénot (at Prémeaux), Moillard.

Hospice de Nuits St. Georges

The hospital was founded in 1692 (the Hospices de Beaune in 1443). The first actual building was the Salle Saint Laurent, followed by the Salle Sainte Madeleine and the Salle Saint Etienne. After the French Revolution, the administration passed from the Augustinian religious order to the mayor of Nuits, at which time two Sisters were appointed to nurse the thirty-six in-patients. During the nineteenth-century special attention was paid to tubercular patients and further extensions were made; as tuberculosis was gradually beaten, the administration of the Hospice changed direction towards geriatric care. The Hospice now takes very special pride in its quite peaceful facilities for the old and poor. Starting with twelve beds in 1692, they now maintain 166.

As with the more famous Hospices de Beaune, the Hospice de Nuits has been aided by gifts of vineyards from local benefactors, whose names are given to the various *cuvées* of the Hospice wines. It was only in 1938 that the Hospice administration first decided to offer their wines of the 1937 vintage by auction. The encouraging results of the first auction were interrupted by the Second World War and only in 1962 did the foundation again auction its wines to the public.

By the 1975 vintage there were fifteen *cuvées* of Nuits St. Georges named and offered by auction. The wines are offered by *pièce* (the Burgundian cask, holding approximately 288 litres), and these fifteen wines were offered in twenty-six lots, a total of 72 *pièces*. It is possible to find these different Nuits St. Georges wines on lists in the U.K., but they are much less well known than the *cuvées* of the Hospices de Beaune.

Vosne Romanée

When you leave Nuits St. Georges, drive north (on RN74) and immediately look out for the sign Vosne Romanée indicated to the left; it is preferable to take the first vineyard road but, if you do miss the turning, don't worry, as there are two other opportunities slightly further along.

In order to study the Vosne Romanée vineyards, which surround the village like jewels, you really should have as detailed a map as possible, because it is essential to appreciate the way in which the vineyards fit together and are placed on the ground. If you can, buy the Larmat *Côte de Nuits*. It costs a little over 20 francs at the time of writing: you will usually be able to get it in Nuits St. Georges or Beaune and, after using it on the spot, it looks good framed when you get home.

The atmosphere of Vosne Romanée is charged with associations, memories and expectations—heady stuff for the wine lover. A short stop in one of the lanes will help you to appreciate the importance of where you are and concentrate the mind onto this village, in which there are clustered together five vineyards internationally venerated, plus several others that are world renowned. Very little ordinary wine is made in the area of this village, as the geography, climate and soil combine in the most favourable way to assist the growers in their noble task of maintaining a reputation forged over the centuries.

In Vosne Romanée, one must begin at the top of the scale and consider the vineyards belonging to the Domaine de la Romanée-Conti. They are the sole owners of the site of Romanée-Conti (1.80 hectares), which has an average production of a mere twenty to twenty-five *pièces* per vintage.

The highest praise has often been given to Romanée-Conti wines, and they have an expansive, deep, richness in which both the bouquet and flavour seem to mould into each other, achieving a harmony of power quite unique. They will, of course, live for many years, and in a mature condition the price they fetch is forbidding. However, a few bottles purchased in their youth would be a reasonable treat for a serious collector —this is the kind of 'wine investment' well worth making.

Since the earliest records of the thirteenth century, this tiny vineyard has changed ownership only nine times. The other vineyard solely owned by the Domaine de la Romanée-Conti is La Tâche (6.02 hectares); it yields a more important crop in commercial terms. In the wines of La Tâche there is a tendency to a more velvety flavour, smoother but lighter than is generally found in Romanée-Conti.

Other great vineyards of Vosne Romanée are shared by several proprietors, with the Domaine de la Romanée-Conti remaining among the largest holders.

La Romanée (0.83 hectares) is entirely owned by Liger-Belair, shippers in Nuits St. Georges.

Romanée St. Vivant (9.54 hectares). In the section owned by the Domaine de la Romanée Conti, they still have a few rows of vines pre-*phylloxera* and consequently ninety years old. These aged vines yield little, but their grapes play a significant part as regards quality. In my experience, the perfume of the bouquet contributes to the majesty of this growth, with a lingering backtaste that consolidates the balance. Romanée St. Vivant will be found under several labels, but I would want to be very certain of its provenance before laying out my money, and I would only buy such a wine from a supplier who had my confidence. The reason for this attitude is simple—it is possible for a poor vintage to be offered, the supplier hoping that the name Romanée St. Vivant will do all the selling and cloud the judgment of the buyer.

I mention this particularly with reference to Romanée St. Vivant, as I was recently offered and rejected a parcel of a usually sound vintage that disgraced the name of this noble wine and its *appellation*. Yet I am sure someone will buy it.

Richebourg (7.99 hectares). The wines of Richebourg possibly present a great variety of styles than the other top growths of Vosne Romanée, as this vineyard has the greatest number of proprietors. For this reason, too, Richebourg is more widely sold and will be seen on lists throughout Europe and the U.S.A. In peak condition, the wine is robust, very generous and uncomplicated, which may sound slightly derogatory, but it is not. Class and style capture the imagination in a Richebourg, leaving no doubt that a fine wine has graced your palate.

Apart from the vineyards already mentioned, there are others of outstanding merit.

Les Grands Echézeaux (9.14 hectares). This vineyard is on the south side of the minor road leading towards Vougeot. The wines possess great elegance and delicacy that can be unrivalled, yet they are less well known than they deserve, due to the supposedly difficult name for Britons. Remember it, however, if you can, for an opportunity may arise when a bargain presents itself and you will appreciate Grands Echézeaux as a truly 'grand vin'.

Les Echézeaux (30.08 hectares). This consists of a group of eleven vineyards, partly surrounding Les Grands Echézeaux and on the upper side of the road. Great bottles of Les Echézeaux are not always to be found synonymously with the name and a good vintage date. This is certainly a label that requires some advice before you pay a vast sum in a restaurant. The wine can be a little tough in youth and it will usually benefit from a reasonable amount of bottle age before consumption. In 1977, I would try to drink the 1970 or 1969 vintages. It is a very good *appellation* for laying down in the right vintage as it is the least expensive of all the great growths of Vosne Romanée—perhaps both because of the difficulty with the name and because people may suppose it to be somehow inferior to Les Grands Echézeaux.

Some further vineyards of great repute are: La Grande Rue, Malconsorts, Suchots, Beaumonts, Damaudes. Growers in Vosne Romanée whose labels are widely distributed are: Domaine de la Romanée Conti, Domaine Gros, Domaine René

Engel, Domaine Henri Lamarche, Domaine Charles Noëllat.

The village of Vosne Romanée has suffered on many occasions in past centuries from foreign marauding troops; it was
largely rebuilt following the local fighting during the 1870
Franco-Prussian War. The hundred-year-old buildings now
show signs of dilapidation and, as in most villages, little is
being done to rebuild or repair. The atmosphere of Vosne
Romanée is essentially private: the tourist trade is somewhat
grudgingly welcomed, because the streets are narrow and the
increased traffic of sightseers interrupts the routines of a
working village.

Clos de Vougeot

Continuing along the vineyard road out of Vosne Romanée,
you will find that the land undulates considerably, thereby
providing many small *combes* (coombs) and *coteaux* (small
hillsides). The brushland of the upper Côte seems close, as the
vineyards give way to the trees that grow thickly here and continue upwards to the top of the Côte and over on to the plateau.

It is a landscape that varies very much in detail—every hundred yards reveals a new type of countryside. So, drive slowly;
as soon as the road descends gently, you will see open out
before you on the right the prospect of the Clos de Vougeot
and its vineyard, which stretches right down to the main road
(RN74). The road goes directly behind the buildings of the Clos
de Vougeot. Notice how low the walls are so as to permit an
enlarged roof area: in former times the monks were very short
of fresh water and this style of building, which looks pushed
into the ground, acted as a type of waterbutt for every shower
of rain, and enabled the maximum quantity of rainwater to be
caught and retained. (Some history of the foundation can be
found on pages 6–8, which deal with the wine order, the
Chevaliers du Tastevin.) The Clos de Vougeot was first wall-
enclosed in the twelfth century, but the buildings today date
from the sixteenth century, when the Cistercian Order rebuilt
them around the original and ancient presshouse and cellar.
This is an essential sight for any Burgundy lover, and the giant
beam press, somewhat resembling a prehistoric animal, is
something to gaze at in awe—from this came wines that made
the reputation of the Côte de Nuits. The visiting hours are
9 a.m. to 11.45 a.m., and 2 p.m. to 5.45 p.m. It is closed from
20th December to 5th January.

The history of the Clos de Vougeot begins in the early
twelfth century, when the Cistercians were first given the land,
and it remained in their possession until the French Revolution
of 1789. During this period, this establishment gained a high
reputation for its wine, using what we might consider as a
public-relations promotional programme. Judicious gifts of
wine to the 'right people'—the higher ranks of the clergy,

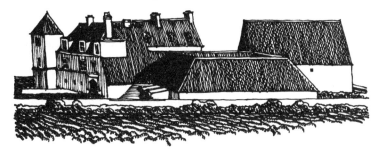

Clos de Vougeot, centre for the Chevaliers du Tastevin

the nobility, rich merchants and the smarter court favourites—drew attention to the quality of Clos de Vougeot. It was a subtle strategy that had great success—the public invariably respond to 'church produce'—even when, as with the Cistercians of the Clos de Vougeot, the makers of the wine officially did not drink it themselves.

After the Revolution, the Clos de Vougeot property was confiscated by the state and auctioned off to one buyer, a M. Focard. Until 1889, the vineyard remained in single ownership, but then it was auctioned off in lots. From this date, therefore, an increasing number of growers have owned portions of the Clos de Vougeot, which has been further divided by the French laws of inheritance which, according to the Code Napoléon, generally mean that property must be divided among all the immediate heirs and which, in consequence, often splits up vineyard holdings into plots of no more than miniature allottment size. It is doubtful if the situation whereby eighty growers have varying shares of a fifty hectare site can hope to produce a uniformly exciting wine. But it is a great status symbol to own a portion of such a vineyard.

The type of today's owners may be divided:

1. The *négociants* of Beaune and Nuits St. Georges who add some glamour to their ordinary business by owning a plot here. Some very familiar names can be found among these proprietors, such as Morin Père et Fils, Pierre Ponnelle, Faiveley, La Reine Pédauque, Champy Père et Fils and Jaboulet-Vercherre.

2. The small grower, usually part of a larger estate (*domaine*), who may sell in bulk to a *négociant* without himself undertaking the bottling of the wine. Hence you will see Clos de Vougeot on many shippers' lists—but they do not necessarily own any vines in the Clos de Vougeot vineyard.

I fear that, before the stricter days of the enforcement of the A.C. regulations, many wines called 'Clos de Vougeot' were sold within the U.K. when their provenance was doubtful. Only now is the quality of true Clos de Vougeot being widely and truly understood on the British market. It is a lush, highly developed wine, with plenty of stamina and a sinewy quality.

Because of the great reputation of Clos de Vougeot—a Burgundy name every drinker knows—it is of supreme importance to buy this wine only from a source on which you can wholeheartedly rely. As each grower has vines of different ages, he may pick at different times, and promote a slow or fast fermentation according to what he thinks is best, the variation of wines that may all be truthfully called 'Clos de Vougeot' is enormous. The good shipper, buying from a selection of these assorted lots, will blend them so that the result is a harmonious, balanced wine, typical of Clos de Vougeot and resulting from the shipper's selection of wines that are both good and able to be satisfactorily married in his blend. This is where his skill—and his reputation—make his name of ultimate significance.

In former centuries it has been told that the monks divided the wines into three qualities from the Clos de Vougeot relative to their geographical position. Wines from the lower ground by the road were called 'Cuvée des Moines'; from the highly favoured middle ground 'Cuvée des Rois', and from the high ground 'Cuvée des Papes'. Stendhal relates the emotional reaction of the French towards Clos de Vougeot when telling of the Revolutionary Colonel Bisson who, marching his troops past the vineyard, required them to 'Present arms', while the regimental band was blazing away. This grand gesture was later imitated by Maréchal MacMahon, who became Duc de Magenta and owned sizable estates in Chassagne Montrachet.

Vougeot

Vougeot is really dominated by its Clos and the remaining vineyard land left over for the village is small. The village itself is of little interest, though the wines of three vineyards will be seen quite regularly on more extensive lists and are well worth trying: Clos de la Perrière, Cras, Clos du Prieuré.

The Domaine Bertagna is probably the best·known estate dealing in these Vougeot wines, and the Beaune shipper Pierre Ponnelle has gained an excellent reputation for his Domaine du Prieuré.

My advice to the traveller following this route would be to visit the Clos de Vougeot and then drive down to the main road in order to look back up the hill and view the Clos and the surrounding vineyards at a distance. Indeed, the building and its vineyard epitomise Burgundy for so many people throughout the world that you should register as many impressions as possible of the whole comparatively small area. At the main road there is a tasting establishment, La Grande Cave, which may be a welcome break.

You should return up the lane alongside the Clos past the entrance to the junction for a right turn. Facing you here is the great vineyard Le Musigny, split into two by a track—but all together it totals only 10 hectares. Ownership is fragmented into ten proprietors, of whom the most renowned is Comte Georges de Vogüë, whose cellar-master Roumier also owns vines in Chambolle and Morey.

Chambolle Musigny

Le Musigny demonstrates the real glory of red Burgundy. When I read what has been written over the last two centuries, I note descriptions of the wine as unique for delicacy, richness of bouquet and majestic finesse. I would not disagree—but the price means that this is a wine for a special occiasion.

It is worth stopping on the road at this stage and noting the contrast of the valueless scrubland above the vineyard with the poor-looking soil of the vineyard itself: it is incredible to think how the worth of the land changes from the intensely valuable ground of the production area to the useless rubble of a mere few feet away. What would this area be without the vine?

The village of Chambolle Musigny can be reached by this secondary road, with the charmingly named vineyard Les Amoureuses on the right side facing that of Le Musigny. Further on, towards the village crossroads, vineyards to the left and right decline in status, apart from that of Les Charmes. On reaching the junction, turn left, up into Chambolle Musigny as this little village, which is unusually situated above the main vineyards, has some most attractive houses and a church noted for some good paintings of saints. If you want a stopping place at this point, I can recommend leaving the village by the D122 signed Curley and, after one kilometre, park off the road so as to enjoy the wooded ravines and rocky, calm countryside.

Our Côte de Nuits tour continues by taking the road out of Chambolle Musigny towards Morey St. Denis. There is a most important vineyard to be seen on the left of the road—Bonnes Mares, which is entitled to its own A.C. as one of the first growths of Burgundy.

The unusual name has never been fully explained, though several suggestions have been made. The one I find most appealing comes from Christopher Fielden, who suggests ". . . it comes from the old Burgundian verb, *marer,* to plough; the vineyard was well tended". Whatever the origin, the wines of Bonnes Mares, which are available from several growers and shippers, please fastidious palates, for they are rich and firm, combining both depth and charm; they develop slowly over the years, reaching a peak at least ten years after their vintage. A Bonnes Mares 1959 of Comte Georges de Vogüë tasted recently ranks among the finest red Burgundies I have tried.

The Bonnes Mares site overlaps into Morey St. Denis, though

this is unimportant, because the wine does not need to mention its village on its label.

The wines of Chambolle Musigny are rated highly by such members of the trade as are able to taste them regularly. Somehow they possess an underlying weight and nobility of flavour that is perhaps unexpected by those who are primarily impressed by their exquisite bouquet and soft fruitiness. I find them fascinating wines, with the particular merit of yielding a range of very attractive smells.

Morey St. Denis

Leaving Bonnes Mares behind, the road leads to the top of Morey St. Denis. Here immediately there is the well known Clos de Tart vineyard on the left. This has remained under a single owner since 1932—the Mommessin family of Mâcon, who are world famous for their Mâconnais and Beaujolais wines. Clos de Tart is fairly widely listed and reaches fairly high prices, but its style will only appeal to those Burgundy drinkers who prefer pale wines of fruity youth, as this particular wine does not seem to have the longevity of its neighbours.

The wines of Morey St. Denis often represent excellent value as against the highly inflated prices of some of the masterpieces previously mentioned (which too frequently simply sell to those with a lot of money who just want to 'drink the label'). The character of the Morey wines is quite definite: power combined with magnificent bouquet. A number of vineyards have become sufficiently well known (apart from Clos de Tart) in increasing the reputation of Morey St. Denis. These are: Clos St. Denis, Clos de la Roche, Clos des Lambrays and Les Sorbets. Before the delimitation of village *appellations*, the wines from Morey were often sold as Gevrey or Chambolle, so until recently they never had the chance to build their own reputation.

Apart from growers such as Roumier, whose Clos de la Bussière has a regular following, a recommendation can be made for those wines purchased by Bouchard Père et Fils and Chanson Père et Fils.

Gevrey Chambertin

After Morey St. Denis the vineyard road is clearly signposted 'Circuit des Vins de la Côte de Nuits'. It goes towards Gevrey Chambertin, whose boundary is crossed soon after leaving Morey. The road descends towards Gevrey Chambertin, where there is an impressive line up of first growth vineyards on both sides. Stop and look about if you have time.

On the left there are: Latricières Chambertin, Le Chambertin, Chambertin Clos de Bèze, Mazis Chambertin, and Ruchottes Chamberlain (above Mazis).

On the right: Mazoyères Chambertin (now sold as Charmes),

Charmes Chambertin, Griotte Chambertin, and Chapelle Chambertin.

The ownership of these vineyards is extremely varied and it has been my experience they are capable of giving exquisite bottles. The Charmes Chambertin has the largest production and will consequently be found more often. If one offers some general tasting notes, they must be taken in the correct context—one person's tasting opportunities can vary greatly from those of others, and writers sometimes risk generalisations about wines without giving the circumstances. To me, the wines of the Chambertin first growth vineyards have a rather heavier and more aggressive character, that is most appealing if they accompany the traditionally rich Burgundian cuisine. I find they are very much the '*goût anglais*', as the U.K. market has always preferred Burgundies with weight and dark colour.

The folklore surrounding Napoleon claims Chambertin was his daily wine during his days of supreme power. Some Paris merchants took a most ignoble business advantage of this after the Retreat from Moscow in 1812 by offering 'Chambertin Retour de Moscou'—it probably had never travelled further than the Halle aux Vins.

As if Napoleon as its champion was not enough, Gevrey Chambertin was also the home of Gaston Roupnel, the poet who gave to Burgundy the same fervour as the rather more eminent poet Frédéric Mistral gave to Provence. One example of his lyricism about Gevrey Chambertin will suffice: "It blends grace and vigour. It unites firmness with power, finesse and delicious differing qualities that compress together an admirable synthesis of unique generosity and of complete virtue".

The history attached to the Chambertin Clos de Bèze and Le Chambertin dates back to the seventh and thirteenth-centuries respectively, though both vineyards are now discussed together. They lie next to each other—and, strangely, such are the irrationalities of the labelling laws, the wine from the Clos de Bèze can be called Chambertin, but not the other way round.

Apparently the success of the monks at the Bèze vineyard caused a M. Bertin to buy the adjacent field, which in time was compressed from Champ de Bertin to Chambertin.

From the thirteenth century to the French Revolution, the Clos de Bèze remained in the same ownership, the Chapter of Langres, but the name of Chambertin was placed firmly on the commercial market by a M. Jobert, who, at the beginning of the nineteenth-century, introduced it throughout the courts of Western Europe by a leasing arrangement that he made on very advantageous terms.

There is now a first-class restaurant, the Rôtisserie de Chambertin, where the finest growths can be drunk amid sumptuous surroundings, yet the cost of a visit here is really very expensive. Up behind Gevrey, there is a special, ancient part of the village, leading into the Combe de Lavaux; here the vineyards of St. Jacques and Cazetiers produce wines of the higher order. In this part of the village I recommend a visit to the Château (it is open from 9.15 a.m., 10.15 on Sundays, until noon and from 2 p.m. to 5 p.m., and there is not charge). Its origins are in the tenth century, it was restored in the thirteenth, and has many features of local interest.

If you have time, follow the D31 out of the village, through the Combe de Lavaux, and climb towards and across the plateau for about six kilometres; the views are beautiful.

Apart from the vineyards already mentioned, Gevrey Chambertin has some very fine second growth wines, which will probably be seen regularly. They are: La Combe aux Moines, Les Champeaux, La Petite Chapelle, Varoilles.

Gevrey Chambertin has a second section of the village called Les Baraques, astride the main road RN74. Against all the labelling rules, the classified vineyards of Gevrey stretch over the road on to the plain and down to the railway. Amongst the sites, the wine of Clos de la Justice, belonging to Pierre Bourée, is one of my first memories of fine Burgundy. It seems to have dropped out from lists in recent years, possibly being a casualty of the direct trade of the increasing 'grower-to-consumer' market that has become a nuisance to the trade distributors. Throughout Gevrey Chambertin there are many distinguished growers. Those whose names are often seen on lists include: Armand Rousseau, Drouhin-Laroze, Camus, Bourée, Domaine Varoilles. Among the *négociants*, Pierre Ponnelle, Faiveley and Joseph Drouhin always keep excellent wines from the village and its great growths.

Brochon and Fixin

To leave Gevrey Chambertin, follow the usual signs marked Brochon and Fixin, but do be careful to take the higher road from the top end of the village in order to see the vineyards from the most favourable vantage points. You will soon arrive at Brochon. The village has no *appellation contrôlée* of its own and its wines are used in the blend for Côte de Nuits Villages on account of their vigorous character. A few vineyards abutting on Gevrey Chambertin are entitled to the latter name. A modern château built in 1900 by the poet, Stephen Liegeard, has been converted into the local school. But this writer is better remembered for creating the title 'Côte d'Azur' in one of his works.

The next village, Fixin, has also its tiny place in the Napoleon legend. Captain Noisot, of the Imperial Guard, was overcome by the departure of Napoleon from Fontainebleau in 1815 after the Hundred Days, when he bade a dramatic farewell to the Guard in what is now known as the Cour des Adieux. Noisot purchased land in Fixin and in 1846 created a park, called after him, with a statue by Rude, 'The Awakening of Napoleon'. As a piece of sculpture it is charged with emotion—perhaps, though, the figure of Napoleon is somewhat bovine to non-French eyes. Near the Parc Noisot is a small museum containing some worthwhile souvenirs of the imperial campaigns. Visits can be made between 9 a.m. and 12.30 and from 1.30 p.m. to 7 p.m.

As a wine village, Fixin has now regained some of its stature from the time when it was the leading vineyard site of the former Côte de Dijon. After the dreadful *phylloxera* plague of the 1870s, Fixin wines were rarely used under the village label, as they were bought for blending with those of Gevrey Chambertin and others. However, even during this period, the vineyards Clos de la Perrière and Clos du Chapitre always retained their reputation and kept the name of Fixin from wholly disappearing.

Fixin gained its village A.C. in 1936, whereafter its fortunes began to improve. By the 1960s, it could claim to have recovered, with *négociants* taking an interest in listing Fixin as a lower priced Côte de Nuits wine. The attraction of Fixin wines seems to be their special depth of flavour, showing an earthy taste that will appeal to the Burgundy drinkers favouring the larger and coarser styles. Personally I have enjoyed a number of Fixin wines and, in addition to the two vineyards mentioned earlier, I suggest readers look out for: Clos Napoléon, La Mazière, Les Hervelets.

In La Mazière the proprietor, Dr. Marion, had some very old wines of the early 1900s. His wine reflected this age by its dark colour, intense bouquet and sturdy backbone, that reached its perfection in both the 1971 and 1972 vintages. I hear that a lot of replanting was started in the late 1960s, and it will now take a few years for the wine made from these younger vines to gain its concentrated taste. The same grower has a small, highly prized section of the Chambertin site.

Fixin is the last village officially within the Côte de Nuits, but the vineyard road does not come to a definite end but enters the suburban mass of Dijon.

Marsannay La Côte

Marsannay, which suffered from the economic depression after World War I, has fought back by producing the only decent rosé wine of the Côte d'Or. The 'Pinot Noir' grape skins are allowed only a short contact with the must, just enough to tint the juice a lively rosé, that enchants the palate by its fruitiness. It is one of the few rosé wines that can be taken seriously: this is not intended to be derogatory to all other rosés, but the rosé of Marsannay has the depth to withstand the heavy sauces of the Burgundian kitchen. Most of the production comes from the

Cave Coopérative and from Clair Daü, one of the most famous domaines in Burgundy, who have vineyards in all the favoured sites of the Côte de Nuits.

Chenôve

This is the last calling point of interest. There was a time when Chenôve enjoyed a fine reputation for two red wine vineyards, Clos du Roi and Clos du Chapitre. But the sole interest now is to visit the Cuverie des Ducs de Bourgogne and to see two magnificent presses of the fifteenth-century, one called 'Big Maggie' after Marguerite, Duchesse de Bourgogne. It is said she had a great capacity—for wine or what? The press was able, it is said, to produce wine to fill up to a hundred pièces at one pressing. (Visits from 8 a.m. until 12 noon, and from 2 p.m. until 7 p.m.)

This is the end of the wine road that has taken the traveller through the greatest wine names of Burgundy. It is a journey to be considered calmly, digested and remembered. Don't hurry it. If you have little time, plan to cover only a part of the route. You will not regret one hour of the circuit.

Côte Chalonnaise Itinerary

In the last ten years, the four village appellations of the Côte Chalonnaise have become far more familiar to those watching wine merchants' lists in the U.K. These villages are Mercurey, Montagny, Rully and Givry. Of these, Mercurey is the acknowledged leader, and several maps and authorities now refer to the Région de Mercurey as a group title, as opposed to Côte Chalonnaise, the name that recognises the neighbouring town of Chalon-sur-Saône.

Whichever overall name one prefers—and either or both may be used—the region can best be approached from Chagny, which itself is an easy twenty minute drive south from Beaune. Chagny has no particular attractions, yet can be a pleasant stopping place for the night because of the Hôtel Lameloise, which is gastronomically renowned. Other small hotels, both in the two and on the outskirts, are perfectly adequate and modestly priced, but the restaurant at Lameloise is very special.

If the area is to be explored thoroughly, perhaps by the visitor already familiar with the Côte d'Or, Chalon-sur-Saône would be an interesting base from which to drive out into the Côte Chalonnaise. Chalon-sur-Saône has a busy and varied centre, with broad boulevards; the shops are probably better stocked than those in Beaune, although Beaune has sprung into life in the last year or two to cope with the growing affluence of both the tourists and the '*habitants*'. A few minutes at the Musée Denon (see Michelin Bourgogne, page 68) will be of interest, as here is exhibited equipment and documentation of the pioneer of photography, Joseph Nicéphore Niépce (1765–1833). He produced the first primitive photograph—a view from his workroom window at Chalon-sur-Saône—in 1822, and later went into partnership with his better-known countryman, Daguerre.

However, for the journey through the vineyards, Chagny will probably be most visitors' starting point and consequently one should leave the town by the RN481.

It should be remembered that the recent increased popularity of the wines of these Chalonnaise vineyards was mainly caused by the price explosion of the Côte d'Or wines during the early 1970s. To some extent, this renewed popularity for the Chalonnaise wines has not been maintained in home and export markets as strongly as the local trade had hoped. My theory is that, when fine classic wines reach prices beyond the average purse, they are not automatically replaced in the consumer's mind by the lesser wines of the same or nearby region, though these may be very similar in style. It seems as if the customer, however conservative he may be, finds it preferable to try something quite different—not risking what, he things, may be something 'second best'.

Geographically, the Côte Chalonnaise is an extension of the Côte de Beaune and therefore of the Côte d'Or. The same grape varieties are demanded by the law of the A.C. and though all Burgundy village *appellations* are given to a broad variety of styles with an *appellation*, it can be stated that the best red Mercurey has sufficient character and nobility to be ranked alongside the Côte de Beaune red wines. In white wines, Montagny will often measure up to an ordinary Chassagne-Montrachet Blanc and will certainly keep company with Auxey Duresses, St. Romain and St. Aubin.

The four villages of importance that give their name to the labels line up north to south on the hillsides, facing east in the direction of Chalon-sur-Saône. Despite the renewed interest in this wine region, the names of the villages are still pretty well unknown to the wine drinking public.

Rully

This is the first village on the itinerary. Since 1830, it has virtually been the home of Sparkling Burgundy, following the discovery that the slightly acidic white wines from the hillsides, made by combining the grape varieties 'Aligoté' and 'Chardonnay', were perfect for making into *vins mousseux* (sparkling by the Champagne method of a secondary fermentation in bottle. The big shippers took advantage of the commercialisation and enlarged the trade by sending their own wines to be dealt with: these were not always straight Burgundy, but blended wines, so as to provide a specific and maintained style. This trade does well at the present time, but few of these sparkling wines acknowledge Rully as their source, and they are more likely to appear under shippers' branded names.

Considerable replanting has taken place, especially on the high lands above the village, and owners have increased their production with the intention of popularising the *appellation* Rully. For the white wines, the 'Chardonnay' grape has to live with the risks of hail and frost, which are very prevalent on this Côte. After the vine has survived nature's attacks, the general style of the wine will have a lively fruitiness, producing a clean and fresh sensation on the palate. This is definitely a wine to sample on the spot. The drawback of Rully white wine is its short life—shorter than the greater wines of the Côte des Blancs to the immediate north. By three or four years after the vintage, the freshness of Rully will tire and the toughness become exaggerated.

The vineyards of Rully surround the village, creating a compact impression, where the *vignerons* and *négociants* seem happy to spare more time with the visitor than some of the more fame-affected villages of the Côte d'Or. Its red wines can be charming and attractive, sharing with the white wines the assets of youth.

Mercurey

Soon after leaving Rully, you will come to Mercurey. The vineyards of Mercurey are widely spread through the surrounding villages of St. Martin-sous-Montaigne and Bourgneuf Val-d'Or, which make 95 per cent red wine, with an important annual average production of 125,000 dozen bottles. Because of this quantity, it is more likely that you will find Mercurey under a shipper's label. The shipper (*négociant*) will buy from more than one grower in order to blend, and it is this skill in blending within an *appellation* (village name) that highlights one of the main functions of his task.

Here another thing about Burgundy should be borne in mind. There are some purists, usually amateurs but not wine merchants, who believe that growers' wines are more 'trustworthy' than shippers' wines. After many years of experience, I do not share this view, and my opinion stems from the many growers' wines I have tasted, where the after-fermentation care or bottling standard does not invariably reach a high level, such as someone in the trade now takes for granted in the shippers with whom he deals. Of course, I have found other growers' wines in the oustanding class—but they are a definite minority. In considering the argument of growers versus *négociants*, it is probably best to remain neutral and not take too definite a line that may be based on prejudice or fashion. So taste each wine for its individual merit: do not make up your mind after a glance at the label.

With Mercurey Rouge, it is probable that the style you find on the export market will have plenty of weight and a definite flavour, including some hint of earthiness and iron. The maturity period is relatively short and there is no need to keep these wines more than five or six years after the vintage. In the rerion, it is more likely that current vintages, even that of the previous year, are offered for drinking. There is no harm in that, as it is a good experiment to see whether you enjoy young red wines, bearing in mind that wines in the restaurants and cafés are specifically intended for short-term consumption and not as *vins de garde* (laying-down wines).

A mention of white Mercurey must be made. There is only a tiny amount made, by five or six growers, but the wine is full of character, similar in style to the elegance of Chassagne-Montrachet, and with the firmness of Meursault.

Mercurey as a place has no special appeal, since a busy road passes directly through the village. Perhaps some of this traffic is caused by the growing number of commercial cellars, owned by shippers using Mercurey as a centre for storing wines in cask. In the region of Mercurey, many vineyards are also owned by shippers, some well known to the export trade: Bouchard Aîné, J. Faivelay, Antonin Rodet and Maurice Protheau, for example.

Off the main road, however, the vineyard lanes are quiet and very pleasant for continuing the wine circuit, with many placed agreeably secluded for a stop, either to study the map, draw a cork, take a picture, or have a picnic. But do leave the place tidy—tourists have acquired something of an ill reputation.

From Mercurey, the road RN481 leads down to Givry, with the vineyards to be seen on the right-hand side, behind the village.

Givry

In researching for information on Givry, I discovered some interesting history, for the wines of Givry once enjoyed a reputation alongside those of Beaune and Volnay. The red wines of Givry were formerly well known in Paris and supplied to several of the French courts. Up to World War I, they had a loyal following, but the economic problems of that time caused Givry to fall from favour and it is only in recent years that a revival has been made.

Givry received its *Appellation Contrôlée* much later than the other Côte Chalonnaise villages—in 1946. This meant that, up to that year, much of its wine was sold as Mercurey. Red wines take up 90 per cent of Givry's production. They have no pretence to greatness, but, when I have served them to people unfamiliar with Givry, they have been much appreciated, especially as accompaniments to rich sauces and heavier dishes. Their slightly sharp, almost bitter backtaste can cut through the richness and finish with a flourish.

This style of wine is often used by shippers as a basic wine for their blends when preparing their stocks of Bourgogne Rouge, likely to be marketed under a house label. This is perfectly legitimate and their tightness of style holds a blend together. Givry can also round off early in its life in bottle, so it can be brought to the table without expensive, long-term maturation. If you are visiting the region, the red wines of Givry can offer you another opportunity for trying the lesser-known wines of Burgundy without spending a fortune. Expect from them a little extra acidity—as in the red wines of the Loire valley.

Montagny

This small village—it is hardly a town—is the centre of vineyards, producing white wine only from the 'Chardonnay' grape. Adjacent to it is Buxy, very well known in the world of wine because of its excellent Cave Coopérative, where first-rate wines are made and bought by a number of firms whose standards are exacting, including many in the U.K. No need to look down on a wine from a cooperative when it is like this, and there is no lack of individuality either, because of the way in which the buyers handle their wines after they have bought them. They do the bottling themselves.

Montagny, as previously mentioned, is largely patronised by several large firms of repute, doubtless due to the reliability of the wines made here and to its lack of fashion. As a place, it is very much 'old Burgundy. and, although not particularly picturesque, is typical of a Burgundy wine town—or village—as it has been for generations. So, if you have time, stop here for a stroll, to appreciate the atmosphere.

The wines are dry but, with a little time in bottle, they can develop a fine, full bouquet and a scale of definite, assertive flavours. Montagny needs only two or three years to be at its best, so don't let it get too old and don't be beguiled—as are so many British—by the unsound belief that an old wine is inevitably better than a young one. This is certainly a foolish generalisation, and never more so than when applied to Montagny. The wine of Montagny is the sort of white Burgundy that is still really a bargain buy, and it will give great pleasure, whereas certain other names not only vary enormously according to the publicity the wines receive, but also, if they are taken up and become 'smart' and sought after, notably in the U.S., the price will soar. And, although I regret to say it, the quality of the wines in general may decline. In short the A.C. 'Montagny' still means something that I respect. I hope that the names of these villages will have made an impression, and that the demand for their wines will once more reward the enthusiasm and hard work being displayed by many young *vignerons*, who see in the Côte Chalonnaise a chance to return their region to its former fame.

The return from the Côte Chalonnaise can be made via Chalon-sur-Saône, Chagny and then back to Beaune.

6
The Food of Burgundy

Some years ago I overheard an excited chef/proprietor exclaim *"La gastronomie en France est finie"*. That may be so, but you can still eat very well indeed, and no better than in the province of Burgundy. The opportunities of facing up to the delights of the Burgundian table will be costly unless you have the good fortune to be invited to lunch or dine with a family. It will be of little comfort to those without this opportunity to know that the fine dishes traditional to this area remain alive more strongly in the kitchens of the *vignerons* and *négociants* than in the restaurants, where the menus become more *'touristique'*—aimed at the traveller with more francs than gastronomic sense.

To our generation (obsessed as it is with calories and cholesterol) the culinary history of Burgundy makes staggering reading. Back in the fourteenth century, when the Dukes of Burgundy ruled over the province from the great palace of Dijon, it was quite normal to sit down to the following series of dishes:

Soups: Leek soup with bacon; Broth of chicken.
First Course: Chicken hotpot; Capon.
Second Course: Suckling pig; Lamb and kid pudding.
Third Course: Frogs legs fricassée; Snails; Crawfish in aspic.
Desserts: Pear compôte; Elderberry fritters.

Time has passed and the dishes have become a little more refined, with modern equivalents of lengthy dinners being prepared for the Chevaliers du Tastevin at the Clos de Vougeot and for the Hospices de Beaune dinner on the Sunday night of the auction. A typical menu would read:

> *Le Jambon persillé du Morvan*
> *Les Quenelles de Brochet Sauce Nantua*
> *Gigot d'Agneau Flageolets*
> *Fromage à la Crème*
> *Sorbet Cassis*

The regional specialities most commonly found in the Burgundy restaurants illustrate the immense natural richness and self-sufficiency of the many *départements* comprising La Bourgogne. A short, mouth-watering survey should start the gastric juices flowing:

Jambon persillé: ham in parsley-flavoured jelly.
Oeufs en meurette: eggs poached in red wine served on croûtons, with shallots in the sauce.
Andouilles: tripe sausages.
Jambon de Morvan: raw ham from the Morvan, a wooded hilly region to the immediate west of the Côte d'Or en route for the Loire, hunting and shooting country.
Escargots: fat Burgundian snails served in garlic sauce. Seasonal and imported snails from East Europe are also offered.
Gougère: delicious cheese-flavoured pastry puffs.
Morilles: many dishes are served '*aux morilles*', the local mushroom of the field variety. They have a definite slight earthy flavour.
Poulet demi-deuil: chicken with the breast threaded with slices of truffle.
Boeuf à la Bourguignonne: beef cooked in red wine, with onions, mushrooms and bacon cubes. Particularly favoured with the wines of the Côte de Nuits, such as Fixin, Morey St. Denis, Gevrey Chambertin or Nuits St. Georges. Personally, I find the flatter-tasting wines of Beaune and Savigny-lès-Beaune suitable, as they seem to mop up the power of the beef stew.
Râble de lièvre: saddle of hare cooked in red wine.
Salade à la Bourguignonne: curly lettuce with added garlic and bacon cubes.
Quenelles de volaille: sausages of chicken meat.
Cassis: blackcurrant, often served with meats as extra sauce or in tartlets with pork.
Saucisse en brioche: a sophisticated sausage roll. Can be offered *à la vigneronne* in red wine sauce, or as a thick sausage in loaf-sized cover.
Boudin: blood sausage, the Burgundian version of black pudding.
Coq au vin: chicken in red wine, with usually a very dark sauce. (*Coq au Chambertin* will appear, but what Chambertin?)
Jambon à la lie de vin: a speciality of ham braised in the red wine left over after the cask bottling, which includes wine deposits, or lees, Sensational sauce for soaking up with bread.
Haricots au vin rouge: beans in red wine.
Pouchouse: a fresh water fish stew from the River Saône and more likely to be found in small restaurants by the river. Pike, tench, eel and perch are the four fish, simmered together in a dry white wine of good quality—Mâcon Lugny, Pouilly Fuissé or Chassagne Montrachet have been used in the stews served by my friends, who add cream and plenty of garlic cloves which gradually dissolve in the slow steaming pot.

Cheeses

The Burgundians are all great cheese eaters but there is no regional cheese of note. As elsewhere in France, expect to be served cheese immediately following the meat course. This is a most sensible practice, as it accompanies the last of the red wine or can herald a fresh bottle if the host's pocket can run to it.

The following cheeses may arrive, sometimes laid out on straw or in miniature baskets similar to those used by vineyard workers:

Epoisses: a soft cheese, rich in flavour, that blends well with the fuller red wines.

Chevrotins: tiny individual goat cheeses, with a hard, dry taste.

Rigottes: a variety of Chevrotins.

St. Florentin: a cow milk cheese, rather powerful for the beginner.

Comté: often served by the wine trade to accompany fine wines, and the same texture as Gruyère and Emmenthal. It needs to be fresh, and is best in spring and autumn.

Fromage à la crème: a fantastic, rich, sweet cream cheese dish. It is served in a mound, to which you add sugar and fresh cream, then mix.

It is fair to say that eating and drinking in the Beaujolais has a wider selection of small traditional restaurants and cafés, so I hope the traveller will continue his journey southward to this picturesque region.

The wine villages of the Côtes d'Or are just a little disappointing for their eating places, so I give a list of villages where well-established cafés have given me traditional dishes away from the main towns: Gevrey Chambertin; Morey St. Denis; Savigny-lès-Beaune; Montagne de Beaune; Auxey Duresses and Meursault.

Restaurants

By law, French restaurants must display their menus outside and from this it is possible to ascertain the price bracket of the establishment. Fixed price menus are always available, but be careful of the '*Menu touristique*' or '*Menu gastronomique*', as both will usually be gargantuan and very expensive.

When you are seated and the menu is presented, be sure to study each page. Waiters have a habit of opening the menu without indicating the cheapest meal on another page.

The wine list, more often than not, is displayed inside the menu cover, and is never printed as explicitly as its British counterpart. Vintages are pencilled in and growers'/shippers' names left out completely. Beware of half bottles as the French do not drink them, and stocks are often tired.

If it is of any conceivable interest, my choice of wine always avoids the expensive, but I hold the view that there is usually a bargain on every list. For white wine an Aligoté can be clean and refreshingly crisp. For the red wine my choice in the past has wandered into the Côtes du Rhône or Beaujolais districts, but these *appellations* have all grown steeply in price. So, unless you want a bottle to assist the study of Burgundy wines or can afford over 50 francs per bottle, it is frequently sensible to order a simple Bourgogne Rouge or a Passe Tout Grain. Personally I avoid 'house' red wines as the average quality of *pichet/carafe* wine does not delight my palate. The French certainly prefer drier and more bitter red wines than we are yet forced to enjoy, although doubtless this taste will be forced on us soon.

If you order a fine old bottle, do ask them to decant it. As time is short and the wine cannot breathe quickly enough with the cork removed, to decant makes sense even if the bottle has no sediment. The waiter may give you the supercilious glare only a French waiter can achieve, but stick it out and insist. They always do as you ask in the end. However, to make up for any bad impression the wine service may give, you will find a standard of restaurant service in Burgundy quite outstanding for its friendliness and patience with foreign visitors. It is better to try in French and fail than not to try at all.

As a parting shot, the sauces of Burgundy cooking are usually rich and filling, so one real meal a day is quite sufficient. Fine picnic country between the wine villages should encourage the traveller to aim straight for the excellent *charcuteries* filled with *pâtés, terrines* and *plats cuisinés* (prepared dishes). Buy your picnics in a town—they are always fresher.

Bon appétit!

Wine Tasting

by Pamela Vandyke Price

There is nothing difficult about tasting wine, even if some people suppose it to be a mystery requiring a long initiation process! The aim of tasting is to discover an enjoyable wine, either enjoyable to drink immediately or likely to prove enjoyable after some period of maturation. When you visit a wine merchant's tasting or attend a tasting party, you are most likely to be offered samples of wines that are ready or very nearly ready to drink. When you visit a wine shipper, or anywhere in the region where wine is produced, you are more likely to get the chance of trying wines that are as yet not ready to drink. Indeed, some of the very finest wines do not make pleasant drinking at all while they are growing up and developing and there may be little temptation to swallow them. But although even a very little experience will acquaint you with different things to look out for in different wines at various stages in their development, the basic procedure of tasting is the same.

Wine is a beautiful and interesting commodity—and those who really know something about it and care for it are delighted to share their enjoyment and appreciation with even the humblest beginner as well as with the experienced. So do not be shy of trying to taste seriously. Ask questions and whenever possible try to note down your impressions of a wine *while* you are tasting it—even an hour later, your thoughts will lack precision. Also, if you remember in detail wines that you like or do not like your future shopping for wine is greatly helped. No-one wants to risk being a wine bore or wine snob, but the world of true lovers of wine is wide, hospitable and worthy of exploration.

Tasting Sense and Tasting Room Manners

The tasting room is the heart of the business of any wine establishment. Care is taken to ensure that the wines may be examined as critically as possible, and that nothing should interfere with this. It sometimes disappoints people to find that a tasting room is rather a clinical place, usually with a north light plus very strong artificial lighting, plenty of white on walls and benches against which the colours of wines may be examined, and with at least one sink and possibly several spittoons as well. But the 'picturesque' type of tasting is usually more in the nature of a party and not for the occasions when large sums of money are being allocated to the buying and selling of a firm's wines.

Visitors to the tasting room will naturally wish to conform to what may be described as 'tasting manners', by not making it difficult for anyone else to make serious use of the room either while they are there, or immediately after their visit. Scent and strongly smelling toiletries for men as well as for women should ideally be avoided or, if someone has just used scent or been on the receiving end of some pungent preparation at hairdresser or barber, it is worthy mentioning the fact by way of excuse, to show that you are aware this may be a distraction. Don't start to smoke, unless specifically invited to do so, as this may make the tasting room unusable for some while, though if the occasion is not too serious the host may well offer cigarettes in his office, if not actually in the tasting room. Beware of thinking that the shallow metal or enamel cups that often stand about in tasting rooms are ashtrays—they are tasting cups, and should not be casually used!

SHARING GLASSES

At professional tastings, unless someone has a cold, mouth infection or anything that obviously necessitates them keeping a single glass for their own use, it is usual for everyone tasting to do so from a single glass, which will be standing either in front of the bottle from which the tasting sample has been drawn or on a space marked in some way on the tasting bench. Some people are hesitant about sharing a glass, but may be reminded that wine is the second oldest disinfectant in the world. If you are really disinclined to taste from a glass used by anyone else, you should make no bones about asking for one for yourself.

Obviously, a woman does not want to leave lipstick on a wine glass at any time—it looks particularly revolting—and even a slight trace can affect the taste of the wine for anyone coming afterwards in a serious appraisal of wine. But it is a very simple matter to wipe the mouth before tasting, should anyone really be at the stage when they leave traces of lipstick on every eating utensil (quite unnecessary, if lipstick is correctly chosen and applied). Men should be reminded that, if they use stronglysmelling soap to wash their hands, or make use of pronouncedly fragrant aftershave lotion or any preparation for hair, they will make the glasses smell just as much as any woman's cosmetic.

A final piece of advice which may seem a little severe though is not so intended: anyone who is trying to form a precise opinion about a wine being tasted requires to be able to give that wine undivided attention. Anyone who, with a false idea of making themselves agreeable, insists on breaking in on the train of thought of the taster at such a moment, peering to see what notes have been written (the experienced taster usually evolves a shorthand which is quite indecipherable to anybody else) and generally making a noise of superficial or frivolous conversation, is likely to be more of a nuisance than a welcome guest in the tasting room. There are plenty of opportunities for asking questions and exchanging points of view without interrupting someone seriously at work, and—in case it should be thought that I am being unnecessarily stern—I must point out that some of the visitors to a tasting room may be those to whom the opportunity is both illuminating and of the greatest importance as regards their future approach to wine. To interfere with an opportunity that may come only rarely, or prevent someone from taking as much advantage as possible out of an experience of serious tasting is both selfish and boorish. The professional may be able to taste on another occasion: the visiting amateur may be deprived of a unique experience by the misplaced bonhomie of someone who really simply wants a drink and would therefore be better to cut short his visit to a tasting room and await the next stage of the proceedings outside.

SPITTING

In an age when virtually any subject can be discussed, it is astonishing that people still display hesitancy and even squeamishness about spitting out samples of wine that they are tasting. A moment's reflection will indicate that to spit out when tasting is the only sensible thing to do: not merely will the mixture of a number of different wines be confusing to the palate and probably upsetting to the stomach, but some samples may be out of condition, others, especially very young wines, undergoing some form of fermentation, and none of them may actually be enjoyable to drink. Spit them out. It is perfectly possible to eject wine from the mouth discreetly and without fuss. If you are tasting samples drawn direct from casks or vats in a cellar, it is usually acceptable to spit on the floor—remember that, if this is stone or cement, there will be some splashback, so try to avoid getting wine on your shoes or those of your companions. In the tasting room, the sink or spittoon will be sluiced down at intervals, even if there is not a tap running to keep everything fresh. Let me reiterate: spit out any samples offered for tasting, unless you are specifically given a portion of wine and advised to drink it. To swallow tasting samples risks giving yourself a stomach upset and will not improve your knowledge or experience of wine.

First Look at the Wine's Appearance

A tasting sample will only occupy a small space in the glass. Its appearance has much to reveal. Ideally, the glass should be perfectly clear and clean and on a stem, though in some regions you may have to make do with small tumblers or possibly a tasting cup of a special type.

The wine should be clear and bright, with something 'living' about it. Do not be concerned that there may be bits (known as 'flyers') in it, as these may be particles from a cask sample, which subsequent filtration may well remove. Their presence, very often, indicates a quality wine, and therefore they are not reasons for condemning the wine in any way.

Tilt the glass away from you at approximately an angle of 45° and hold it against something white, so that you can examine the colour. The living quality should be obvious, rather in the way that the water of a spring is different from the flat dull water drawn from a tap and left to stand for several days. Whether the wine is red or white, it should be pleasant, ideally beautiful to look at and give pleasure to the eye.

What the Wines Indicate by Colour

WHITE WINES

These tend to deepen in colour as they age, and, usually but by no means invariably, the sweeter wines start their life by being more golden than the pale light lemon gold of the drier wines. It is also fairly safe to generalize to the extent of saying that white wines from warm southern vineyards usually start by having a more yellow-straw colour than those from very cold vineyards, which will be pale lemon yellow, or almost very pale green. A really old white wine (old in terms of its own maturity, not specifically related to its age in terms of years) may assume almost an orange tinge, reminiscent of some of the dry Madeiras; this, and the sort of smell and taste that can come off such wines result in the term 'maderised' often being applied to them. It does not mean that they are undrinkable by any means, but they will have changed their character.

Look, too, at the actual consistency of the wine in the glass. The way in which it clings to the sides of the glass and trails downwards with the pull of gravity can indicate a wine of great quality if these trails (known as 'legs') are marked. This is also indicative of the glycerine content which will be marked in the wines that naturally contain a certain sweetness.

RED WINES

Red wines tend to grow paler as they age, many of them being purple-red at the outset. It is probably easier for most people to see the different tones of colour in a red wine and it is helpful sometimes to know that, with a very fine wine (whether you like it or not) there tend to be far more distinct tones of colour visible as you tilt the glass than in even a good cheap wine. Look at the 'eye' of the wine at the centre of the liquid, and then see the gradations of colour out to the edge where the wine meets the glass: a young red wine will be purplish down to black, with a rim that may begin to lighten almost to a deep lilac tone. With a little more maturity, it may become reddish and in the end a beautiful crimson-orange with great age. Red Bordeaux probably lightens more throughout its life than red Burgundy, which tends to be very purple at the outset, except in certain years when the colour can be on the light side.

Remember that, with all wines, age is relative. Some wines show signs of great age when they are young in years, simply because they are wines that should be at their peak while comparatively young and fresh; others, including the very greatest red wines and certain whites, remain apparently youthful for many years. Unfortunately, today's economic pressures make it necessary for many wine-makers to be able to mature their wines faster than in the past, so as not to tie up their capital; this means that a wine which you may have heard of as taking a long time to mature can be at its peak years before you expected this.

Caution is advisable when appraising wines solely by colour, simply because the control of wine-making these days is a very skilled matter and has rightly been judged as important in the appeal a wine makes to its public. If you doubt this, get someone to prepare you two samples of the same red wine, one of them having some additional colouring in it, put there either with culinary colouring matter or by the addition of a few drops of a much darker wine. You will be surprised by the way in which you feel the darker wine to be more 'full-bodied' and possibly 'fruity'! Similarly, if you think that colour does not influence taste, try giving a critical appraisal of a wine out of a glass that is a dark definite colour, such as blue, green, or black: you will be astonished to find how, once one sense used in tasting is cut off, all the others are somehow distorted.

Smell the Wine

A wine should have a pleasant healthy smell, which, in certain wines, can be complex but which should always give enjoyment. You will release this and be able to sniff it more easily if you circulate the wine in the glass, holding the glass by the stem or, possibly, by the foot (not as difficult as it looks at the outset) and simply swinging the liquid round, putting your nose into the glass at intervals and sniffing. The aeration of the wine releases the fragrance.

Surprisingly, very few wines actually 'smell of the grape' although people often wish that they might! A few grapes, notably the Muscat, do possess a distinctive aroma, which is quite often easily identified as 'grapiness', but otherwise although certain grapes may result in wines smelling of those grapes, the associations with fruit are not always obvious. A wine should smell fresh and clean, but there are certain smells which, with young wines, may be present for a short time, indicating nothing more than that the wine is going through a phase of natural development.

These smells include the slightly beery smell which may mean the wine is still undergoing a stage of fermentation, a vaguely yeasty smell, which sometimes seems present when a wine has recently been bottled, a slightly sharp smell, often described as 'green', which may be present in even the best made wine in a year when the grapes have been unable to ripen perfectly. Or, in some instances, this green smell may mean that the vineyard contains a high proportion of young vines, the use of which is apparent in the early stages of the wine's development. Obviously woody smells can mean that the wine has been matured in new wood, this smell passing with time also, or, if the woodiness is of a soggy sort, it may mean that there is a faulty stave in the cask in which the wine has been matured.

You are unlikely to find 'corked' wine in a sample of a very young, bottled wine, but a complete absence of smell can be slightly sinister in this respect, indicating that something is preventing the wine from giving off its fragrance. It is the 'swimming bath' smell, reminiscent of chlorine, that is for me most definitely associated with corkiness—which, by the way, has nothing whatsoever to do with bits of cork being in the wine. Some people do find that corkiness reminds them of the smell of cork, but I have never been able to see this myself. A musty smell can be indicative of an ill-made wine, but it should not be confused with 'bottle stink'. This is the smell (that is often stale and flat) of the little quantity of air held in the bottle of wine under the cork, which may affect the taste of the first portion poured. A little aeration will cause this to pass very soon.

The good smells, interesting and pleasing to the nose, include a type of fruitiness, the different sorts of which will be associated with the various types of grape when the taster has gained a little experience. Young wines, especially those that are most enjoyable when drunk fairly young when they are at their peak of freshness, usually have an obvious fruity smell. Then there is a crisp almost sharp smell, like the freshness of a good apple, which can indicate the right kind of acidity balancing the fruit. This should be noticed in most young wines, especially those that are dry and light. Wines from cool vineyards tend to have more smell than wines from hot ones. The infinity of delicate, flowery, herby, and subtle depths of scent with which some of the great German and other northern vineyards are associated, and in the reds from vineyards where the vine has to struggle, such as Burgundy and Bordeaux, can be so beautiful, even while the wines are very young that, as is sometimes said, 'it is almost unnecessary to drink when the smell is so fascinating'.

With the finest wines, try to break up the general impression made on you by the smell into the first impact, anything that then reveals itself by further aeration, and finally see whether there appears to be some subtle, as yet unrevealed fragrance underneath the other smell. Wines are like people in this respect, the more obvious are not always the most rewarding. Sometimes, right at the end of a tasting, a smell can come out of a wine glass that may indicate something to look forward to in the future. Try to remain alert to register this if it is there.

Taste the Wine

Always adapt tasting techniques to what experience has taught you suits your own abilities best. But the most usual way to taste is to draw a very small quantity of wine—about a teaspoon-ful—into the mouth, accompanied by a small amount of air. There is no need to make a loud sucking noise while doing this, but the circumstance of pulling the wine into the mouth, plus some air, seems to sharpen up the impression it can make. Then circulate the wine in your mouth, pulling it over the tongue, letting it run along the sides of the mouth and getting a general 'feel' of what it is like: light/dry/sweetish/thick/ thin/assertive/reticent/chewy/attaching itself to the sides of the mouth/attacking the gums (everyone's gums tend to ache after a lot of tasting!) Try to split up the numerous impressions which the wine may have to give you before you spit it out. Don't be hesitant about taking more than one sample in quick succession.

AFTER-TASTE AND FINISH

When you have tasted the wine and have spat out the sample, breathe out sharply—you will be aware of an extra smell, rather than a taste, that passes across the palate. This is the after-taste and it can reveal quite a lot about the wine: for example, it may be far more definitely fragrant than the original bouquet or smell, or it may have a lingering quality, known in wine terms as 'length', both of which can indicate that the wine has great promise and may develop considerably. Or there can be little or no after-taste, when a wine may be described as 'short'.

The way in which the wine leaves the palate is the 'finish'. Does it finish cleanly, or has it a trace of stickiness? Has it a final flourish of flavour, a definite extra touch of taste, or does it die away rapidly? The finish of any good wine, regardless of price, should be clean, and, with a fine wine, entice the drinker to take more. With a modest type of wine, the finish should at least refresh rather than cloy the palate.

THE WORK OF TASTING

Some people really do not like tasting young wines, and affirm that there is no point in doing so, as they are going to enjoy them when the wines are grown-up. This is quite true, but any musi-cian or artist is fascinated to see someone in the same line of business rehearsing or working. The way in which wines develop is equally fascinating; and, even though no-one would claim to know exactly what a wine was going to be like at its peak, any more than even the most experienced human being could judge of the detailed progress of another human's performance, the attempt to relate experience to what a wine is saying at one time or another and the backing of one's own judgment in hazarding a view as to the evolution of a particular wine is one of the most engrossing and challenging exercises. Make no mistake, tasting is hard work. It requires great concentration and results in real exhaustion if you have subjected yourself to a long session. The fact that it is, to a wine lover, perhaps the most exhilerating pursuit of all, is a compensation.

Remember what a particular wine has to give: a wine that should be dry ought not, in general, to lack acidity and be seemingly too sweet. A wine that is meant to develop over a period of years need not always be very amiable or even give very much impression of what it is going to be like, when it is in its early stages. A very fine wine usually makes some impression on the taster, though all wines can go through phases when they seem to smell and taste of very little. The medium priced and cheap wines are very difficult to taste: they can risk being very much alike, and experience is necessary to differentiate between their attributes and what may be their deficiencies.

Don't bother yourself with the game most wine lovers play of getting friends to 'taste blind' until you are a little experienced. It is perfectly true that this can be great fun and teach you an enormous amount, as the stark appraisal of a wine about which you know nothing at all can be a great test of your own honesty, courage and relation of the power of your taste memory. The fact that some people, on some occasions, can identify a wide range of wines with complete accuracy, is not, by itself, a tribute to more than the luck of the day and their considerable experience; they can be equally mistaken, with reasons for being so, on other occasions. The beginner can easily be discouraged by making apparently pointless mistakes, so that it is wise not to indulge in this until you have a little general knowledge of wines.

Meanwhile, it is only sense to bear in mind that you are unlikely, for example, to be offered a range of red Bordeaux in the tasting room of a Burgundy shipper or vice versa! Nor, in one wine region, are you likely to be offered a wide range of wines from several other districts. The visitor to Bordeaux who was disappointed in not seeing where 'the sherry wines were made' is not unique! Although a firm may handle a vast range of wines, it is unlikely that the visitor will ever be asked to taste more than one type at a time. What they are offered over a hospitable table, of course, may be very much wider in scope.

Taking Notes

Notes made on the spot are far more valuable than any general impressions recorded even a short time afterwards, but it is extremely difficult to translate taste impressions into words. To put 'good' or 'bad' is really equally useless—how do you know? It may simply be that the wine in question does or does not appeal to you at that stage of your experience. Try, whenever possible, to differentiate between wines that you truly like and wines that you may admire as good but which do not particularly appeal to you. I would recommend any taster to make up his or her own set of tasting terms as far as possible. It is useless making play with technicalities only half understood from books or to use terms which may mean something to one taster but very little to another. With even slight experience, it is possible to translate your own tasting impressions into language that may be generally understood, but if it helps you, for example, to write 'carnations' or 'violets' against a particular type of wine, then do so. You associate this wine with those particular flowers and no-one else is obliged to do so. But, if, merely because someone who seems to be authoritative, insists that 'wild thyme' or 'scrubbed oak table' is inevitably associated with a particular wine, do not attempt to agree with them unless you can wholly associate yourself with the experience—it is worthless if you cannot share it, and your own impressions will be more valuable to you if you can make the effort to formulate them in terms that enable you to remember what you taste.

Always date your tasting notes and be precise about where the tasting was done, if you are not using a tasting sheet provided by the establishment. It is surprisingly easy, especially if the wines are good and seem to become better and better, for the impression at the end of any tasting to be wonderful but confused!

Deterrents to Tasting

There are a few things that make it difficult to taste. Some—smoking, scent, etc.—have been mentioned earlier. Obviously, a cold prevents you from doing so easily, and very few people find it easy to taste after they have had a large mid-day meal. The morning, when the stomach is fairly empty and both the mind and body are fresh, is probably the ideal time. Otherwise, if you wish to prepare your palate for serious tasting, remember that violently flavoured or piquant foods can make it difficult for you, and this should also be remembered when you are choosing wines to go with a meal. Of course, few people would be silly enough to eat curry, large amounts of pickles, or anything containing a high proportion of vinegar while trying to drink a fine wine, but other things can impair the receptivity of the palate, notably eggs and chocolate. Indeed, a single chocolate makes it almost impossible for me to taste for several hours afterwards! Anything very sweet, or a piece of confectionery, will also make it quite impossible to taste for some time—even a medium dry wine will taste incredibly acid after such a thing.

People are sometimes offered crusts of dry bread or biscuits to refresh the palate at a tasting, but there is one thing that you will never accept if you are being serious about the procedure—cheese. Not for nothing do the wine trade say 'we buy on apples, sell on cheese', because the alkalinity of cheese has the effect of making almost any wine taste better than it may perhaps be, whereas the acidity of an apple, or a crisp young carrot, will show up a wine quite brutally for good or bad.

APPENDIX 2

Glossary of Wine Terms

Whilst most of the major shippers and guided tours will have 'English spoken' visits, it may be helpful to list some of the expressions that could be met on a cellar visit where only French is spoken. From these adjectives and nouns it should be possible to find a suitable description after tasting a wine or to ask a sensible question during a tour of the cellars when wine making equipment can be seen.

The odd intelligent remark dropped into a conversation or tour will probably prolong the discourse by the enthusiastic response from your host, and give you a little breathing space before putting the next French sentence together. To those visitors fortunate enough to have mastered the French language, a fair sprinkling of these words will take the vineyard proprietor or *négociant* into a most serious discussion. Please do not take these words as a definitive list; only the more common words are presented in this guide.

If the situation arises where French is the language of the visit, do remember that it is polite and quite normal to shake hands and state your name—nine times out of ten they will forget it, but don't worry, you have tried.

Tasting Terms

Amer. A bitter taste of excess tannin—can indicate long living wine.

Austère. Austere—a wine lacking charm.

Bouchonné. A 'corked' wine—the cork has become mouldy and imparts an 'old socks' smell. If this is slight, it will ease when open to the air. If it is heavy, it's undrinkable.

Bouquet. The smell of the wine.

Caractère. The overall impression given by the wine, bearing in mind where it originates.

Cassis. Blackcurrants—occasionally red wine can have a slight overtone of this flavour.

Complet. A well-made wine, with all the necessary constituents of quality.

Corps. Relates to the weight of the flavour in the mouth, too much, or too little.

Corsé. A full-bodied wine without necessarily any distinction.

Coupé. Blended.

Dégustation. A tasting—often seen as a sign outside a house or cellar to encourage buyers in to taste. Be prudent—this may mean you will be expected to pay or buy some wine.

Dur. Hard in flavour—more noticeable in young red wines.

Fin. Fine in the sense of being distinguished. Will apply to any wine outstanding in its class.

Finesse. My personal adjective to describe breeding of wine.

Frais. Chilled.

Fruité. Fruity. In both red and white wines, the fruitiness is tasted as a first impression.

Généreux. Big fat wine, but pleasing, shows its youth and grapiness.

Goût. Taste. Used mostly as part of an expression, for example: *goût de bois* (woody taste); *goût de ferment* (yeasty); *goût de miel* (honey flavour, found in some mature dry white wines); *goût de terroir* ('earthy'—a taste given to some wines by the soil, noticeably mostly in red wines. When excessive, it spoils the balance).

Madérisé. White wine going brown from age or early oxidation—unpleasant.

Mûr. Ripe taste. An excessive fruitness can indicate a very hot summer and picking conditions during the harvest. The term can apply to red and white wines.

Piqué. Sour.

Plat. Flat, uninteresting style.

Plein. Full in flavour.

Sec. Dry.

Séché. Dried-out flavour.

Sévère. A harsh, abrasive taste.

Souffre. Sulphur—the standard sterilising agent for wines, casks and vats, and used in white wines to stabilize and prolong life. If overdone, the smell comes nastily through—it can tickle the throat and make the taster cough.

Souple. Supple—a wine yielding gently all its flavour.

Tannin. Tannin. An essential organic constituent of wine derived from the roots, stems, pips and grape skins dissolved during fermentation. Noticeable mainly in the red wines, it acts as the fortress of the wine during youth and eases off during maturation. Tastes astringent, dries out the mouth.

Tendre. Tender—applicable to young red wines, the softness of which develops quickly after bottling.

Vigoureux. An attacking flavour.

Vin de garde. A wine to lay down several years to mature slowly towards its peak (literally 'a wine to keep').

Vineux. A wine high in alcohol—enough to spoil it.

Velouté. Velvety, smooth rich style. Term applied only to red wines.

Wine-making terms

Acide acétique. Acetic acid, which is always present in wine—in excess, it makes the wine taste of vinegar.

Cave. Cellar.

Cep. Individual vine.

Cépage. Any grape variety.

Chaptalisation. A procedure named after Dr. Chaptal (early nineteenth century). It is permitted in Burgundy to add sucrose (sugar) to the must prior to fermentation if the must is deficient in sugar, so as to increase the final alcoholic content by up to an extra 2°. This practice is still hotly debated, but in many cases does permit the grower to improve the balance of his wine.

Climat. Any particular vineyard—i.e. site.

Clos. An enclosed vineyard, usually surrounded by a wall. If the word is used on a label, the wine must come only from the particular vineyard.

Collage. The fining of the wine, to maintain clarity and remove unwanted skins, etc.

Cru. Growth—describes an individual vineyard of some standing, often classified.

Cuve. A vat used either for fermentation, or for blending, or storage.

Dépôt. A deposit found in red and white wines after maturing—this sediment is left behind in the bottle when decanting.

Domaine. Vineyard(s) belonging to the same proprietor. 'Mise en (or du) Domaine' or 'Domaine Bottled' indicates wine bottled by the proprietor, but not necessarily at the vineyard (as is signified by 'château bottling' in Bordeaux and elsewhere) but in the domaine cellars. Many domaines have vineyards in several villages, centralising their fermentation, storage, bottling activities in just one cellar.

Egrappage. Removal of the grape stalks prior to fermentation.

Fleuraison. Flowering of the vines in the spring.

Grand vin. A term which means nothing at all, but is sometimes seen on a wine list in an attempt to enhance the appeal of a wine.

Haut. High.

Hectare. 2.471 acres. Vineyard areas are quoted in hectares (abbreviated to 'ha').

Lie. Lees or sediment in cask or vat.

Marque (déposée). Registered trade mark or brand name for standard and basic wines, used by shipper for sales continuity.

Millésime. The vintage date as on the label.

Mise. The bottling.

Moût. The must—crushed grapes and their juices before fermentation.

Nature. Still wine.

Ouillage. Ullage—the process of regular topping up of casks and vats to replace evaporation.

Ouvrée. An old Burgundian vineyard measure of 0.0428 hectare.

Panier à vendange. A straw basket used by grape pickers. A special shape peculiar to Burgundy.

Pasteurisation. A process named after Dr. Louis Pasteur (1822–95). The wine is heated to between 130° and 170°F. to destroy all micro-organisms and stabilise the wine. A few Burgundy shippers adopt this practice for cheap wines, but not for fine wines as it arrests all development.

Pichet. A carafe or jug for wine in restaurants, containing around 50 cl.

Pièce. The oak cask used in Burgundy, holding 228 litres (around 24/25 cases of 12 bottles). The generic English word is 'hogshead'. The equivalent name in Chablis is *'feuillette'*.

Pot. A special Beaujolais bottle of slender, globular shape, containing 46 centilitres. The firm Piat in the Beaujolais have registered their name for their particular bottle.

Pressoir. The press used for crushing the grapes at vintage time.

Réserve. A meaningless term, used to dress up the description of a wine by implying superior quality.

Récolte. The harvest.

Soutirage. The process of racking or drawing off the clear wine into a fresh cask or vat, leaving behind the sediment, during the period of maturation in wood.

Vin mousseux. A sparkling wine, qualified on the label as being made either by the 'Méthode Champenoise' or 'Produit en Cuve Close'. The former applies only to mousseux with appellation (as Bourgogne Mousseux A.C., *Méthode Champenoise*).

Further Reading

Allen, H. Warner, *Natural Red Wines*, Constable, 1951.

Arlott and Fielden, *Burgundy—Vines and Wines*, Davis Poynter, 1976. At the time of writing, the most recent publication. Combines the eloquence of John Arlott and the Burgundy trade background of Christopher Fielden, former export director of Chanson Père et Fils.

Gwynn, Stephen, *Burgundy*, Constable, 1934. Can sometimes be found in second-hand bookshops.

Gunn, Peter, *Burgundy, Landscape with Figures*, Gollancz, 1976. Essays on the history of the region, interesting to any traveller.

Johnson, Hugh, *World Atlas of Wine*, Mitchell Beazley, 1971. Ideal geographic study and some help with names of leading growers.

Lichine, Alexis, *The Wines of France*, Cassell, 1956.

Lichine, Alexis, *Encyclopaedia of Wines and Spirits*, Cassell, 1967. Excellent for technical and general information. Some opinions read like facts.

Marrison, L. W., *Wines and Spirits*, Penguin, 1973 (3rd edition).

Michelin, *Maps 66 and 70*.

Michelin, *Green Guide—Burgundy*. Available in English.

Poupon and Forgeot, *The Wines of Burgundy*, Presses Universitaires de France, 1974 (revised and updated). The two French masters of Burgundy. Basic details and concise information in an English translation by Edward and Michael Ott.

Shand, P. Morton, *A Book of French Wines*, Penguin, 1964 (revised by Cyril Ray). Originally published in 1928 and information now out of date, but excellent wine reading.

Sichel, Allan, *The Penguin Book of Wines*, Penguin, 1965 (revised 1976).

Speaight, Robert, *The Companion Guide to Burgundy*, Collins, 1975. Very good as an historical survey and about places to visit.

Vandyke Price, Pamela, *Eating and Drinking in France Today*, Tom Stacey, 1972. Detailed and sensible information.

Waugh, Alec, *In Praise of Wine,* Cassell, 1959.

Yoxall, H. W. *The Wines of Burgundy*, International Wine & Food Society, 1968; Penguin, 1974. Written with great feeling by a true lover of Burgundy.

Appellation Contrôlée in Burgundy

The general principle and philosophy of the laws governing the production of Burgundy wines are covered by a system of protection, both for the growers and consumers alike, that falls within the title '*Appellation Contrôlée*.

There are six main types of controls that have to be scrupulously observed before a wine can claim the relevant 'A.C'. These, in brief, are:

1. The delimited geographic area of production. (From this the wine's title will be taken—for example, the *appellation* 'Beaune' has 540 hectares of vineyards allotted a potential A.C. if the other conditions are fulfilled.)

2. The grape varieties permitted to be grown (see pages 15–18 for grapes).

3. The maximum production of wine that can be made per hectare.

4. The minimum alcoholic degree of the wine. (Again, as an example in the Beaune A.C., red wines must reach 10.5°, and those of *premiers crus* vineyards must reach 11.5° to obtain the A.C.)

5. The treatment to which the wine may be subjected during production and maturing in bulk (in vats or tanks, of wood or stainless steel).

6. The method of cultivation and pruning of the vines.

Until recently, many countries receiving Burgundy wines in bulk for home bottling, such as the U.K., The Netherlands and Switzerland, did not always exactly respect the French laws of A.C. This could work to the advantage of the British drinker. For example, suppose more wine than that permitted by the A.C. was made, quite legitimately, in a favourable year: the surplus yield on '*rendement*' (the official quantity declared each vintage) could be sold, without the A.C., to a British shipper, who was then able to label it with the name of the vineyard from which it did indeed come—and pass on the benefit of the lower price he paid to the U.K. consumer. Happily, these abuses are now almost cleared away as the Common Market laws do not permit a non-A.C. wine to carry an A.C. label (which has greatly reduced bottling of Burgundy A. C. wines outside the region). It is, however, also fair to say that wines which may be 100 per cent genuine as far as the A.C.s are involved, need not be 100 per cent fine drinking—which is even more reason to know something about Burgundy and from whom you buy it.

THE A.C. LAWS

As applicable in Burgundy, these break down into four categories:

1. The Generic/Regional Appellation.
2. The Village Appellation.
3. The Village/Vineyard Appellation.
4. Single Vineyard Appellations.

An explanation of these categories will help to clarify the various labels met on the merchant's list or in restaurants.

GENERIC/REGIONAL APPELLATIONS

Bourgogne Grand Ordinaire. This is the lowest A.C., dealing with any red, white or rosé wines from the specified area of Burgundy. The grape varieties are: (for red/rosé) 'Gamay', 'Pinot Noir', 'Tressot' and 'César; and (for white) 'Chardonnay', 'Pinot Blanc', 'Aligoté', 'Melon de Bourgogne', 'Sacy'.

Production of this quality of wine is no longer important because some of these grape varieties individually gain higher *appellations*. Mostly found in local restaurants, Bourgogne Grand Ordinaire is rarely sold with a vintage attached to it, as two vintages are usually blended to attain a pleasant balance and to make a wine for quick consumption.

Bourgogne Passe-Tout-Grains. This is an A.C. for both red and rosé wines, but it is applied almost exclusively to red wines made from a blend of wines produced from a mixture of grapes in the proportions of two-thirds Gamay and one-third Pinot Noir. It can be pleasant when young and fresh, but a few years' bottle age helps the marriage of two wines along and makes it even better.

Bourgogne Aligoté. This concerns only white wines made from the Aligoté grape. In good summers, these wines achieve a balance of fruit and acidity, and they are ideal for apéritif drinking. Aligoté is the best wine for making a *vin blanc cassis* (Kir), see page 33. Some villages have become well known for their Aligoté' quality—for example, Pernand Vergelesses, Savigny and Bouzeron, also the Hautes Côtes de Beaune et Nuits.

Bourgogne. An A.C. which covers red, white and rosé wines. These wines are becoming important, in these economically restricted times, for the Burgundy drinkers of the British Isles. From this appellation some very decent wines can be purchased, if your merchant can establish their origin—and, of course, if you like them. After all, no matter how grand the name on the label, it is the enjoyment of the wine in the bottle that is the really important thing!

The red wines must come from the classic grape Pinot Noir,

or they may be made from the Gamay grape if they are produced in the nine senior villages of the Beaujolais region (which is outside the scope of this book). For the white wines, only the Chardonnay or Pinot Blanc grapes may be used.

The production of red and white Bourgogne A.C. can be boosted by some village wines being either produced in excess of the permitted limits, or by being found lacking some of the conditions demanded by a village A.C. certificate. As an example, I have said that Beaune A.C. must reach 10.5°; so, if a Beaune reaches only 10°, it can be declassified to be called Bourgogne. Would you notice the difference? I doubt it, if the wine was sound and well made.

Bourgogne Hautes-Côtes de Beaune; and Bourgogne Hautes-Côtes de Nuits. Both these little known appellations exemplify the story of a renaissance of wines, gathering pace and beginning in France to fill a certain gap in the Burgundy wine trade. It is yet to be seen if these A.C.s can mean much to wine drinkers outside France.

The geographical area of these two appellations is best studied on the map (there is one in the booklet *Beaune—Hautes Côtes et Côte de Beaune*, available at l'Office du Tourisme opposite the Hospices de Beaune in the town centre. The vineyards contributing to the two appellations lie on the plateaux and higher ground of their respective Côtes.

Chablis. This regional *appellation* is discussed in full on pages 48 to 54.

VILLAGE APPELLATIONS

In the table following this chapter the various Burgundy appellations are broken down by category, so as to show at a glance the standing and distribution of any wine name or label that you may see. Village appellations are precisely as described—that is, the wine name on the A.C. label will come from the specific vineyard to which the near by village has given its name. From these lists, all the world-famous Burgundy wine names can be traced.

The delineation of these village appellations must have caused joy, resentment and sometimes cynical apathy, according to who owned what. Ancient village/parish boundaries were ignored and attention to the lie of the land, known wine qualities and historical reference were the deciding factors for the I.N.A.O. (*Institut National des Appellations d'Origine*—the body which determines the A.C.s). Even so, some minor anachronisms remain. For example, Santenots is a fine red wine vineyard nominally in Volnay but largely in Meursault, but the whole production (within the A.C. limits) is entitled to be called Volnay Santenots (not Meuresault Santenots). As another example, but of slighter importance, the dividing line between the A.C. limits of Puligny Montrachet and Chassagne Montrachet goes straight through the middle of the greatest vineyards, both Le Montrachet and Bâtard Montrachet.

These village divisions also create, simply by force of nature, varying size of areas with appellations, so that Beaune has a 'surface' or area of vines of approximately 540 hectares, with an average crop of 9,300 hecto-litres. Pommard, its neighbour, has a 'surface' area of vines of 340 hectares, yet produced an average 10,500 hectolitres. Going down to the smaller villages, tiny Monthélie, next up from Volnay, has only 93 hectares of vines, producing 2,050 hectolitres. So it will be appreciated that one A.C. may be well known simply because its area is such that a lot of wine can be made—or vice versa.

At this village level of *appellation contrôlée*, one may see a grower's label or a *négociant*'s label—which brings us to another point. Growers' labels for a village *appellation* do not necessarily indicate that the wine comes from a single vineyard, because growers may own several plots in the same village from which they may blend the wines for the village A.C. Of course, the style of vinification is the same—in some cases all their grapes will ferment together, in others they keep the different lots separate to blend later during maturation in wood. *Négociants*' village wines will usually be a blend of wines from various growers.

Côte de Beaune Villages. This appellation is quite different from that of Côte de Beaune. It is used for red wines only, which attain a minimum degree of 10.5°, coming from sixteen *appellations* of the Côte de Beaune. For this A.C., the wine must be a blend of two appellations or more from: Dezize-lès-Maranges, Cheilly-lès-Maranges, Chassagne-Montrachet, Puligny Montrachet, Meursault, Auxey Duresses, Chorey, Saint Aubin, Santenay, Meursault-Blagny, Monhélie, Savigny-lès-Beaune, Ladoix, Pernand Vergelesses. Obviously the blending is the total arbiter of the eventual style. Perhaps the general characteristics will be a robust, generous flavour, needing three or four years' bottle age to show at its best.

Côte de Beaune. Now rarely seen, this appellation covers small parcels of vineyards above Beaune on the Montagne. Do not confuse it with Côte de Beaune Villages.

Côte de Nuits Villages. Five villages combine to make up this *appellation* but only one, Fixin, has its own village appellation. The villages are: Fixin, Brochon, Prissy, Comblanchien, Corgoloin. The *appellation* is mainly for red wine which must reach 10.5°. Formerly this appellation was called 'Vins Fins de la Côte de Nuits'.

Crément de Bourgogne; Bourgogne Mousseux. These A.C.s are really old flames under new names. Bourgogne Mousseux was thought to be a non-commercial title for a sparkling wine, so in 1975 the *appellation* Crémant de Bourgogne was created. The basic requirements are that the wine must be made by the '*méthode champenoise*' and be appellation Bourgogne Blanc, of which 30 per cent must come from the noble grape variety, Chardonnay. Otherwise the Aligoté is used because of its suitable acidity, a requisite for quality sparkling wines. If a stand-in for Champagne is needed, then the sparkling wines of Burgundy can be the next best thing, but beware—many sparkling wines are made in the Burgundy region from wines brought in from other districts; they do not have a Burgundy appellation yet the shipper's name and address will give the impression that they are sparkling Burgundy—until you study the label.

Village/Vineyard Appellations

There is no classification of Burgundy vineyards with the same historic and commercial significance as the 1855 Paris Exhibition classification of the Gironde (Bordeaux), but several authoritative attempts have been made to distinguish the various grades of quality from the Côte d'Or Vineyards. Basically, there are three classes of vineyards:

Grand Cru	Great Growth
Premier Cru	First Growth
Deuxième Cru	Second Growth

There have been classifications down to Third Growths, but these have mostly disappeared. First and Second Growth wines are the subject of this section.

In the case of *Premier Cru* (First Growth) vineyards, the name of the village plus the vineyard name must appear on the label in the same size of lettering or type. For example: Beaune Bressandes. Premier Cru or 1er Cru may appear also if wished by the source of supply. The name will be followed on the label by the words 'Appellation Contrôlée' or again if wished 'Appellation Beaune Bressandes Contrôlée' or even 'Appellation Beaune 1er Cru Contrôlée'. If a grower or *négociant* blends two *Premier Cru* vineyards together from the same village, he loses the right to the vineyard names as far as the A.C. is concerned but is permitted to state on the label 'Beaune 1er Cru', for example. For *Deuxième Cru* vineyards, the name of the village must appear twice the size of the vineyard name. For example: 'Beaune Belissand, Appellation Beaune Contrôlée'. In practice, very few *Deuxième Cru* vineyards are now offered under the vineyard name, as the village name is sufficient for the wine market.

Vineyard Appellations

Here we arrive at the top of the tree (or vine!). The *Grands Crus* are the most excellent and highly prized vineyards in the world. Because of their distinction, these vineyards are entitled, within production limits, to announce their names on the bottle without making reference to their village. For example: 'Bonnes Mares, Appellation Bonnes Mares Contrôlée'. Here the Bonnes Mares vineyard actually extends over the boundary between the village A.C.s of Chambolle Musigny and Morey St. Denis in the Côte de Nuits.

In the white wines, there is the example of the vineyard Le Montrachet in the Côte de Beaune, that is half in Chassagne and half in Puligny—but no matter; neither village need be acknowledged on the label.

In some instances, the *Grand Cru* name has been craftily attached to the village name to add lustre and with perhaps an eye to business. Hence Chambolle Musigny, where the village of Chambolle added that of Musigny, its most renowned vineyard. Nuits took St. Georges to itself in 1892, but alas the famous St. Georges vineyard was not nominated as one of the thirty-one *Grands Crus* by the I.N.A.O. in the 1937 classification. For that you have to look for a label 'Nuits St. Georges Les St. Georges'.

If the opportunity ever presents itself to you to taste or consume a bottle of *Grand Cru* Burgundy, do take your time and, as with all fine wine, do not rush the experience. These wines have a lot to say for themselves and will not be hurried. They deserve calm, lesurely appraisal.

Much of the more specialist information relating to the laws of A.C. will be seen in the chapter dealing with the way in which Burgundy is made (page 15ff). However, there is one word often heard and read—'declassification'—that can be a mystery unless the production limits are understood in relation to the A.C. With the increase of technical assistance available to the *vigneron*, the average quantities produced in the Côte d'Or began to rise. Burgundy sales improved, but the laws of A.C. allowed most Côte d'Or villages the top limit of making 35 hectolitres of wine per hectare, and this resulted in some considerable excesses above the permitted quantities, for perfectly good reasons. Up until 1974, the laws allowed the growers to declassify these extra quantities downwards to lower *appellations*; thus a grower, say, in Pommard who made 40 hectolitres of wine from one hectare of vines would be allowed to declassify five hectolitres to A.C. Bourgogne Rouge. In really abundant years the A.C. authorities did permit certain A.C. increases, such as in 1973, when the 35 hectos limit was increased to 45 hectos.

These production limits had not been satisfactory from many points of view for some years. By 1974 new legislation was ready for enactment and a new system of production control was introduced. In future, the A.C. authorities will, after consultation, announce the annual permitted levels per hectare following the harvest. Each grower will be granted an extra 20 per cent over this figure but, to gain the full *appellation*, he must submit his wine for approval within a short time of the harvest. But there is a snag: if his sample is not considered suitable, he loses the *appellation* for the whole of his stock. I should not like to be present when a grower hears of this latter fate! For, obviously, a wine only permitted to bear an A.C. that is lower in the *appellation* scale is unlikely to fetch the price of an A.C. graded higher, however good the wine itself may actually be.

There are certain more complicated aspects of this quantity control that will be without interest for the reader. The description as I have given it brings out the basic concept—the new regulations do allow higher levels of wine production but also, for the first time, some quality control is exerted.

These laws of protection and encouragment are not perfect, but without them the wine trade would be a nasty free-for-all and muddle. My very minor overall criticism is that A.C. establishes a social order of vineyards and, thereby, a price structure. It is too easy for famous *appellations* to fetch a price above the real tasting value of the wine and this price is kept up by a world demand, lacking in information about the true relative merits that can change rapidly over a short succession of vintages. All this is yet another reason why you should drink the wine and not the label—however famous the name on it may be.

List of Burgundy A.C.s

Bourgogne Rouge	Generic/regional
Aloxe-Corton	Village
Auxey-Duresses	Village
Bâtard-Montrachet	Vineyard
Beaune	Village
Bienvenues Bâtard-Montrachet	Vineyard
Blagny	Village
Bonnes Mares	Vineyard
Bourgogne Blanc	Generic/regional
Bourgogne Aligoté	Generic/regional
Bourgogne Hautes Côtes de Beaune	Generic/regional
Bourgogne Hautes Côtes de Nuits	Generic/regional
Bourgogne Marsannay La Côte	Rosé—village
Bourgogne Passetoutgrains	Generic
Chablis	Regional
Chambertin	Vineyard
Chambertin Clos de Bèze	Vineyard
Chambolle-Musigny	Village
Chapelle Chambertin	Vineyard
Chassagne-Montrachet	Village
Cheilly-lès-Maranges	Village
Chevalier Montrachet	Vineyard
Chorey lès Beaune	Village
Clos de la Roche	Vineyard

Clos de Tart	Vineyard
Clos de Vougeot	Vineyard
Clos Saint-Denis	Vineyard
Corton	Vineyard
Corton Charlemagne	Vineyard
Côte de Beaune	Generic/regional
Côte de Beaune-Villages	Generic/regional
Côte de Nuits-Villages	Generic/regional
Crémant de Bourgogne	Generic/regional
Criots Bâtard-Montrachet	Vineyard
Dezize-lès-Maranges	Village
Echézeaux	Vineyard
Fixin	Village
Gevrey-Chambertin	Village
Givry	Village
Grands Echézeaux	Vineyard
Griotte Chambertin	Vineyard
Ladoix	Village
Latricières Chambertin	Vineyard
Mazis-Chambertin	Vineyard
Mazoyéres-Chambertin	Vineyard
Mercurey	Village
Meursault	Village
Montagny	Village
Monthélie	Village
Montrachet	Vineyard
Morey Saint-Denis	Village
Musigny	Vineyard
Nuits-Saint-Georges	Village
Pernand-Vergelesses	Village
Petit Chablis	Generic/regional
Pommard	Village
Puligny-Montrachet	Village
Richebourg	Vineyard
Romanée	Vineyard
Romanée Conti	Vineyard
Romanée Saint-Vivant	Vineyard
Ruchottes-Chambertin	Vineyard
Rully	Village
Saint-Aubin	Village
Saint-Romain	Village
Sampigny-lès-Maranges	Village
Santenay	Village
Savigny-lès-Beaune	Village
Tâche, La	Vineyard
Volnay	Village
Volnay Santenots	Vineyard
Vosne-Romanée	Village
Vougeot	Village

Index